The Ruby Mirror
and other essays

Lisa Williams Kline

THE BRIDGE

The Bridge
Huntersville, N.C.

Acknowledgments:
The author gratefully acknowledges the editors of the publications who first published these essays:
Blue Crow Publishing, "Parasailing With My Daughter"
Carolina Woman, "Writing Test"
Idol Talk, "Good Guys"
Literary Mama, "The Invisible Husband"
Main Street Rag, "Blizzard Babies"
Main Street Rag, "In Sickness and in Health"
moonShine review, "Gladiator"
Novello Festival Press, "Ornament Custody"
Novello Festival Press, "Hundred-Year-Old Welsh Christmas Pudding"
Personal Stories Curiosities Anthology, "Dancing Holes in Her Shoes"
Personal Stories Trouble Anthology, "The Trouble with Mating Season"
Sasee, "An Old Couch, Two Chairs, and Covid"
Sasee, "A Lifetime of Wardrobe Malfunctions"
Skirt, "Happy Points"
The Writer, "Don't Give Up"

Author's Note
This book is a work of creative nonfiction. While I've tried to portray events as accurately as possible, I've recreated conversations and summarized scenes. Some of the names of people and identifying details have been changed in order to protect their privacy.

ISBN 979-8-9857250-0-1
Published by The Bridge, www.TheBridgeBooks.com
Huntersville, North Carolina
Original cover by Kelsey Kline Mard and design by Diana Wade

for Jeff,
Caitlin and Josh,
and Kelsey and Seph

ALSO BY LISA WILLIAMS KLINE

Eleanor Hill
Princesses of Atlantis
Write Before Your Eyes
Take Me
Summer of the Wolves
Wild Horse Spring
Blue Autumn Cruise
Winter's Tide
Season of Change
One Week of You
One Week of the Heart

Contents

I

My Mother's Prophecies

Good Guys

I didn't sit at the "cool" lunch table at Wiley Junior High. I was not in the seventh-grade in-crowd, so I wasn't in on the plan that was concocted against our Spanish teacher, Señor Valderas, until the very last minute.

Someone came up to me after lunch that day and said, "Every time Señor Valderas turns his back to write on the board, one person is going to go out the back door of the classroom, and then everyone else is going to move down one seat until nobody is left in his class. Pass the word."

On the way to my locker, I became quite anxious trying to decide whether to participate. First, I was a devoted rule follower, terrified of getting into trouble. I had once participated in a coordinated pencil drop and found myself drenched in cold sweat. Second, and most important, my favorite show, *The Man from U.N.C.L.E.*, with my idol, Illya Kuryakin, was on that night, and if I got into trouble I might not be allowed to watch it.

Every week, my brother and I had to receive special dispensation from our parents to stay up past our bedtime to watch the escapist tongue-in-cheek spy series.

"Illya Kuryakin!" I squealed at the beginning of the show each week, with swooning seventh-grade drama, giving his name the flourish of the character's alluring accent.

"Napoleon Solo!" my fourth-grade brother shouted with equal zeal. We'd throw ourselves on the floor, our chins in our hands, a few feet from our small black-and-white set (everyone else in the neighborhood had already gotten color), and slip into the world of spies.

Illya Kuryakin's and Napoleon Solo's names had exactly the right number of syllables, and they rolled off the tongue with incredible ease. Now that I'm an adult writer, I have to laugh at the fun those writers must have had creating those mellifluous names.

The writers must have had fun with the acronyms of U.N.C.L.E. and its diabolical nemesis, T.H.R.U.S.H., too. U.N.C.L.E. stood for United Network Command for Law and Enforcement, the international spy organization with headquarters located in the back of "an ordinary tailor shop" in the East Forties in New York City. T.H.R.U.S.H. stood for the Technological Hierarchy for the Removal of Undesirables and the Subjugation of Humanity, which to me today strikes a suddenly more chilling note. Agents from T.H.R.U.S.H. were always kidnapping scientists to get them to do their nefarious work for them.

Each week, Illya Kuryakin and Napoleon Solo executed white-knuckle spy missions while maintaining effortless, deadpan James Bond banter. (Ian Fleming was one of the producers). Illya wore an incredibly sexy black turtleneck with his gun holster buckled over one shoulder. Not only was he clever, resourceful, and unflappable, he had an accent to die for. His character was supposed to be from Russia. He was played by actor David McCallum, and I now realize that his accent wasn't Russian but Scottish. At age thirteen, I didn't notice the difference.

Illya had a lean and wolfish face, with a shock of Beatle-length blond hair. I liked him better than Napoleon Solo, who was too suave for me. Illya was aloof, *mysterious*. He rarely showed emotion. In my mind, his most attractive characteristic was that he seemed a little bit shy, like me. He was not a defector, like Mikhail Baryshnikov; Illya was still a Russian citizen. Yet, could he remain loyal to his mother country and still do his humanitarian spy work? Did he leave a Russian girlfriend behind? These questions were never answered, which only ratcheted up the intrigue. In my fascination with him, I was not alone. David McCallum received more fan mail than any other MGM star between 1964 and 1968, the years when *The Man from U.N.C.L.E.* was on the air.

Even though my brother and I had endured years of school drills, crouching under our flimsy desks in case of attack from our Russian enemies, Illya in my mind could never be a "bad guy." The Russian *government* was our enemy. Illya Kuryakin was a "good guy" in every way, and I could still have a crush on him.

The men from U.N.C.L.E. were always helping the kidnapped scientists escape from T.H.R.U.S.H., but I never had any fear that my father, who was a scientist, would be kidnapped. We lived a serene life on the bucolic Wake Forest University campus in Winston-Salem, North Carolina. Dad had gone to school on the GI Bill after serving on a submarine in World War II. He had seen his share of war and danger, but now strolled across the peaceful green campus to teach his classes and do research in the lab. Our only nod to the Cold War was the fallout shelter in our basement, which Mom at first stocked with canned vegetables. Eventually, it became a cinder-block storage room full of junk. In Winston-Salem, Southern decorum was paramount, but the community was multicultural for a city of its small size. Dad's colleagues in the physics department came from all over the world—India, China, Israel, and the Netherlands—and had multiple religions and accents. Growing up on the college campus, I assumed that people of all nations lived together in harmony, as in the physics department, and I was long an adult before I realized this wasn't true.

I liked reading and writing, and remember studying *Green Mansions* and *Animal Farm* and *1984* and *Lord of the Flies* in English class, with themes of revolution, human rights, and environmental responsibility that I was probably too young to understand. I attended a sort of magnet school that was integrated from the beginning, and I had been taking Spanish since third grade. My foreign-language skills, in spite of my fascination with Illya Kuryakin's accent, were sadly lacking.

That day of the planned escape, as we noisily piled through the door of Señor Valderas's Spanish classroom, there was a palpable, almost breathless, excitement and anticipation. I still had not decided what I was going to do. Watching *The Man from U.N.C.L.E.* was a highlight of my week, and I did not want to endanger that in any way.

"Buenos dias, estudientes," said Señor Valderas in his monotone voice. "Sientese, por favor." Señor Valderas had a beautiful accent. He was pale and balding, and I found it curious that he always wore a shabbily elegant three-piece suit to class while other teachers dressed more casually. His wife, Señora Valderas, taught Spanish at the high school. We heard she was stricter and more vivacious.

Even to my seventh-grade eyes, Señor Valderas's heart was not in the job. He seemed to be in a trance most of the time, inches away from collapsing from exhaustion every day. He often forgot to mark things wrong on our papers and gave us better grades than we deserved. If people were clowning around in the back of the class, Señor would pretend not to notice. He wouldn't even call them down. When it happened, he would turn his back and begin to write long lists of verb tenses on the board. I wondered about this. How could he not notice that one kid was shooting a paper football across the room and yelling, "Heads up, Huffstetter!"? As an adult looking back, I realize that Señor Valderas's lack of reaction could have been a combination of pride and despair. But we were only thirteen.

We waited with bated breath for Señor to turn his back to write on the board. He droned on and on, his despair and hopelessness seeming to envelop him like a cloud as we recited verb tenses. Some of us deliberately stumbled on the tenses just to alert him that we might need extra drills using the board. At last, he turned and picked up the chalk.

There was an audible, collective intake of our breath as the student on the end closest to the door ducked out into the hall. I happened to be in the back row; he seated us in alphabetical order, and my last name was Williams. A few people moved down one seat. Others snickered. Señor did not turn around.

A second person ducked out the door, serenaded by more chuckling, and more people moved down. Everyone seemed euphoric with this escape from authority. An empty seat beckoned beside me.

The kid next to me gave me a meaningful look.

My heart beat like a parade drum. There was much I didn't understand at that time: the difference between a Russian and Scottish accent; the themes of *1984*, *Green Mansions*, and *Animal Farm*;

the inhumane way that so many people around the world over the centuries had been mistreated when I had been so loved. But I did know that I was not a rebel.

I stayed in my seat and continued to recite the verbs. I pretended not to see the exasperated glances of my fellow students.

Someone crawled over me and moved down, giving me a dirty look. A few more people ducked out. I have no idea what they did for the rest of the Spanish period. Went down the hall to the bathroom and smoked, probably. Señor Valderas, when he at last turned back around, gave no indication that he noticed they had left. Aloof to it all, he turned no one in.

But the revolution against Señor Valderas fizzled. There were enough students, like me, who would not leave the classroom that the plot failed. And it wasn't only because I didn't want to miss *The Man from U.N.C.L.E.* on TV that night. Maybe it was because I was a cowardly rule follower. Or maybe, because both of my parents were teachers, I couldn't show a teacher disrespect.

I was not a secretive kid, so that night at dinner, I told my parents and my brother about the scheme to escape Señor Valderas's classroom.

"I bet you chickened out," my brother said.

"How do you know?" I said.

"We know you," teased my father.

It was then that my parents told me that Señor Valderas and his wife had escaped from Cuba when Castro took over. He had been a lawyer, and he and his wife had to flee in the dark of night, leaving everything behind. Teaching Spanish had been the only jobs they could find here. We took the globe down from the bookshelf, and our parents showed us where Cuba was.

"So why did they have to leave?" I asked. In my protected life, I could not even imagine a place so dangerous you'd have to escape.

"I suppose they refused to become communists," my mother guessed.

As I was cleaning up the dishes, I thought about my giddy classmates escaping from Señor Valderas's class that day, and I wondered what Señor Valderas's escape from Cuba must have been like. Did they have to pay someone to take them? Did they get shot at, like the scientists on *The Man from U.N.C.L.E.*? I understood why he didn't turn anyone in. And I had a glimmer of understanding about why he was sad: He missed his home.

"Who's finished with their homework and ready to watch *The Man from U.N.C.L.E.*?" my father said now, scooping chocolate ice cream into four bowls.

"Me!" my brother and I shouted at the same time, and we lay on the floor, our chins in our hands, in front of the TV.

The moment I'd been waiting for all week had arrived. The exciting opening music for *The Man from U.N.C.L.E.* swelled, and we watched Illya Kuryakin skillfully land a helicopter to help a scientist from the international public health service escape from the clutches of T.H.R.U.S.H. As I sat with our family, safely ensconced in our den, beside the green and peaceful campus, with our fallout shelter just below us, I hoped Señor Valderas and his wife had someone like Illya Kuryakin to help them escape from Cuba.

Years later, I would move away from the South and fall in love with and marry a man with a similar family story of escape. His grandfather, Nathan Zagoria, escaped from Russia during the war, in the engine room of a cargo ship, with his little brother Max. Two boys, headed for America, leaving the rest of their family behind. The man who was supposed to bring them food for their journey took their money and left. For days, they licked the sweating water pipes in the engine room to survive. Finally, a crew member found the boys, gave them food, and smuggled them into New Jersey. That brave story is one of the many reasons I fell in love with my husband and his family.

His grandfather's escape reminded me of Señor Valderas's escape from Cuba. Even though Illya Kuryakin was a TV character, in helping people escape from intolerable circumstances, he portrayed values that my family and my husband's family hold dear. Having a crush on a character from a country I had been taught was our enemy helped me to redefine "the good guys" and the "bad guys," which I think has helped me over my lifetime to see the world in a more open way.

My Mother's Prophecies

I was riding with my mother down Stratford Road in Winston-Salem, on our way to buy shoes at the only place in town that carried my small size, when my mom made a prophecy that I'd never forgotten. I'd been telling Mom about my eighth grade crush, Howie Jacobs.

"So he raises his hand in Biology and he asks a lot of off-the-wall, out-to-lunch questions. He's so funny!"

"What kind of questions?" Mom turned to pierce me with her hazel eyes.

I was now sorry I'd brought it up. I could never tell my mother what Howie had actually asked. Which was, "How do you make a hormone?" And everyone in the class had started snickering like crazy. Miss Norben had said, "I know exactly what you're doing, Howie, and you're not going to get away with it! Go stand in the hall now!" So as everyone continued to laugh, Howie, who was short, dark-haired, and wiry, wove through the desks and out into the hall with a self-satisfied smile, giving me a wink as he passed by. My heart sped up and I could feel myself flush. I was a rule follower. I'd never do anything so brazen. I burned with admiration for Howie's off-color antics and irreverence. But my mother would be scandalized. More and more, I couldn't tell my mother everything the way I used to.

"I can't really remember right now but he's just really funny," I finished lamely.

"Is that boy Jewish?" Mom said.

"I don't know. Why?"

"His last name."

"So?" There weren't many Jewish people in Winston-Salem, my small hometown in North Carolina, which was founded by the Moravians in the 18th century. At that age, I had a vague understanding that Jewish people had a different belief system than Christians, but wasn't clear on what it was. Once, I'd gone Christmas caroling in a friend's neighborhood and we'd gone to one house and sung our hearts out and as we were walking away one of the kids said, "We shouldn't have gone there! They're Jewish!" And then we'd all been mortified that we'd offended the people, though they seemed perfectly nice, smiling from the doorway, and not offended at all.

Mom was talking as we navigated the Stratford Shopping Center parking lot, and while I'd been musing I'd missed part of what she was saying. "In fact, I believe you're going to marry a Jewish man, Lisa. And I believe you're going to be married about three times."

"What?" I stared at my mother in disbelief. It never occurred to me that I'd marry someone who didn't share my faith. But I had to admit that Howie believing something different made him seem more interesting to me than other boys I'd met. But my mother was saying I was going to be married three times! I was horrified. My mom and dad had dated for seven years before marrying, because of World War II and Dad's schooling. They considered their marital vows to be sacrosanct. I couldn't for a moment imagine either of my parents married to anyone else. From our nightly family dinners, to our constant competition in family games, to our beach vacations together, to Mom and Dad sitting side by side on the couch watching TV at night, their marriage was the bedrock of my life. I wasn't exactly sure that my life would be like theirs, but I had assumed it might be similar. So why would my mom think that I would be married to three different people? Did she think I'd get two divorces? Or did she think my husbands would die?

"Mom, why would you say that?"

Mom pulled our sensible Honda square back into a parking spot in front of the shoe store that carried size fours. "I don't know, I just think of you as a bohemian sort of person, Lisa."

Was I bohemian? Did that mean loose? Free-spirited? Did that mean my mother thought I was going to have sex with a lot of people? God, this was mortifying. I didn't know what kind of person I was at thirteen, really. I was obedient on the outside but sneaky on the inside. According to my parents, the house could have burned down around me and I wouldn't have noticed if I was reading a book or drawing. I loved reading fantasy, such as the books about King Arthur by T.H. White (*The Once and Future King*), The Narnia series by C.S. Lewis, and *The Hobbit* and its following trilogy by Tolkien. I wanted friends but never called anyone, or made any effort to get together, preferring to make up stories and scribble them down instead. I loved cats. I'd just become boy-crazy. What did that all add up to?

I followed my mother into the shoe store. Mom was petite, and had inherited her Italian father's olive skin and dark hair. She'd been the May queen at Westhampton College when she attended there. I was petite, too, but looked like my dad, with dishwater-blond hair and pale skin that turned beet-red in the sun. Plus I'd always been myopic, and wore thick glasses, choosing cat eye frames with glitter because I thought they looked glamorous. Mom loved to shop, priding herself on being able to track down things that were hard to find, like my shoes. I actually had more shoes than I needed simply because Mom and I always felt that if we found a pair small enough we better buy them.

This store had a whole rack of sample shoes in my size. While this at first seemed like a windfall, the racks revealed very few pairs that were actually useful for daily wear. The ultra-small sample shoes were often off-beat or featured garish colors and heels high enough to break an ankle. The shoes I had to choose from today included shiny green alligator patent leather with square toes, yellow stilettos with white polka dot bows, and high navy pumps with giant clunky red heels.

"Why do you think I'm bohemian, Mom?" I asked, as I tried on the navy ones with the red heels.

Did the fact that Mom prophesied this future with multiple husbands mean it was going to come true? Would I try to obey my mother and *make* it come true? Was she giving me permission to live this kind of life? I have looked back on this desultory conversation I had with my mother during a shopping trip and wondered if it was a weird form of predestination. The statement haunted me. Eventually I buried it somewhere in the back of my mind. Mom sometimes liked to make statements for shock value and I decided that was what this was. I wonder now why I didn't ask Mom what she meant by this, and I believe the answer is that I was a timid, obedient, and introverted young person and often didn't speak up at times when most people might.

"Let's get those," my mother said, without answering my question. I was clomping around the store in the crippling heels. Mom loved anything with a patriotic color scheme.

"Where will I wear them?"

"You'll find a place. It's better to have them than not have them."

And that night a place to wear them materialized. We were all watching *Mission: Impossible*—Dad in his La-Z-Boy, Mom on the couch, my brother and me lying on our stomachs on the rug in front of the TV. The phone on the kitchen wall rang and I raced to get it.

"I'm wondering if you want to go to a dance at the Town Club on Friday night." Howie had a deep voice that didn't totally fit with his short stature.

I almost laughed because I thought everything he said was funny. A dance! With the boy who kept the whole biology class in stitches! Both parents and my brother could hear every word of my conversation unless I stretched the cord around the corner and wedged myself into the living room.

"Can I go?" I put my hand over the receiver and asked my parents.

"Who will be driving?" my dad asked.

"I heard that," Howie said. "Well, I will, of course."

"Oh—"

"I kid, I kid. What do you think? I'm only fourteen. My parents'll drive us."

Was every word out of his mouth not hilarious? I giggled.

I knew my parents would let me go. They were eager for me to have more fun, to have an easier life, than they had when they were young during the Depression and the war. And maybe they trusted me. Foolishly, perhaps. Some girls' parents wouldn't let them date until they were sixteen but my parents weren't like that.

"Be home by eleven," my dad said.

That Friday night, Howie came to the front door, in a small houndstooth sport coat that fit him well. He was wiry, a wrestler, not muscular, but fit and coordinated. His curly dark hair was carefully combed. He surprised me with a lovely white carnation wrist corsage.

"A flower," he announced, thrusting it toward me.

"Oh!" I was delighted, and slipped it over my hand. I was wearing the clunky blue and red shoes, and almost fell trying to get into the back seat of Howie's parents' car. His mother turned around in her seat to ask me questions about my interests in school and about the physics classes my father taught at Wake Forest as we drove to the dance. When she turned back to face the front, Howie put his hand on my knee, which I thought took a lot of guts with his parents right there. I wasn't sure I wanted him to do it, but I admired the fact that he truly had no fear. I didn't move his hand. As a person who lived in fear of even *accidentally* breaking rules, I was smitten with him.

"I like those shoes," Howie said.

I'd have to tell Mom that. She'd be pleased.

After Howie's parents dropped us off, he led me upstairs to the dance, in a small room at the Town Club downtown, with a round wooden dance floor and, in an alcove off the main room, a table with a long white tablecloth and punch and snacks. Everything felt a little odd because I didn't know anyone else and it didn't appear that Howie did, either. The band was great, playing a lot of Temptations songs like "Ain't Too Proud to Beg." Howie was a good dancer. After taking off the new shoes, I was also able to dance. We took breaks to try the punch, and Howie joked about spiking it, though he didn't, and I carried my clunky shoes around by the straps.

"A minister, a priest, and a rabbit went into a bar. The rabbit said, 'I think I'm a typo.'" Howie kept up a banter that left me weak with laughter. I laughed all night. When it came time to go home, it was painful putting the shoes back on.

Standing on my front porch, with his parents waiting in the driveway, Howie pulled me to him and gave me a hard kiss with no slobber.

"I want to give you my Camp Tel Yehudah pin," he said, with sudden inspiration. "And I want you to wear it right . . . there!" At that he pinched my nipple.

I was so stunned I couldn't even react. With his parents right there! My mouth fell open and my boob tingled. Howie bounded down the front steps and slid into the back seat of his parents' car and before I could slap him or even ask what was Camp Tel Yehudah he was gone.

I was so shocked by what Howie did that I forgot to tell my mother that he had said he liked my shoes. That night I lay in bed reliving the evening and that bizarre moment. What had it all meant? Did Howie like me? Was he making fun of me when he pinched my boob? Was the whole evening a joke? Girls in high school were wearing guys' pins, but they weren't pins from summer camps, they were athletic pins. Who ever heard of a pin from a summer camp? Maybe Howie was making fun of the whole idea of pins. Maybe he was making fun of me.

But I would never know. Howie never asked me out again.

Mom had a flamboyant older half-sister named Blanche, and she was the antithesis to my mother. While Mom was a hard-working and serious teetotaler who always wore a sensible cloth coat, Blanche smoked, drank whiskey, dyed her hair Marilyn Monroe blond, was fun-loving with a gravelly and infectious smoker's laugh, and wore furs.

Blanche married a Jewish man in Richmond, Virginia, in the 1940s. His name was Maurice Salomonsky, and they had two sons. Maurice was the man who walked my mother down the aisle when she married my dad, since Mom's father had passed away when she was seven. Mom was fond of Maurice; he had been kind to her. Mom used to go to Blanche's house to spend afternoons and Maurice showed interest in her education. Blanche had agreed when she married Maurice that she'd raise the boys Jewish, and she did, but Blanche never converted and attended a protestant church all her life. After Maurice died, Blanche married another Jewish man named Maurice, which was certainly a funny coincidence. He converted to Christianity, and they lived together happily for many years until he, too, died.

My mother and Blanche didn't see each other often, possibly because Blanche was fourteen years older than my mother, and they hadn't really grown up together. The first time Blanche came to our house for a visit when I was thirteen, I was transfixed.

Blanche swept into our modest house, with her bottle-blonde curls, wearing spike heels, a low-cut dress, and waving a long cigarette. "Dahlin', it's your Aunt Blanche, come here and let me give you some sugah!"

I sidled up, sniffing the bluish cigarette smoke, which I found glamorous, as I'd started sneaking them myself, blowing smoke out the bathroom window. I let Blanche pull me close to her ample bosom. Having Blanche in the house would be fun. For one thing, she had a loud voice and a belly laugh and told outrageous stories. She was bigger than life. For another, it would make it easier for me to sneak more cigarettes.

"We thought you'd never get here!" my mother exclaimed. I could tell that my father and brother were fascinated by Aunt Blanche but that my mother was a little embarrassed by her raucous sense of humor. That afternoon Blanche put on her parakeet-yellow two-piece bathing suit (I had never seen my mother wear anything but a modest black one-piece) and went in our backyard and slathered her somewhat sagging body with baby oil, lay on a lounge chair, read a women's magazine, and smoked. Our neighbor must have taken out his trash three times that afternoon, craning his neck to peer through the trees. Nobody in the faculty neighborhood at Wake Forest sunbathed. They were all inside grading papers, preparing lectures, or doing research. When, the next day, my mother took Blanche to Old Salem, Winston-Salem's historical tourist area, Mom reported that Blanche flirted her way around the meticulously restored centuries-old homes, tottering down the cobblestone streets in her spike heels, and all of the retired men who were historical guides practically fell over themselves trying to open doors for her.

We didn't have a guest room at our house, so Blanche slept in the extra twin bed in my bedroom. When we got ready for bed, I put on my flowered flannel nightgown, trying not to watch as Blanche put on a diaphanous lacy thing that barely hid her tanned body.

"You ought to show off that figure more, sugah."

I thought I would die of embarrassment. I choked out a "Thank you," slid into bed, and pulled the covers up to my ears. But then I thought, *I ought to?*

I wondered, during Blanche's visit, about my mother's prophecy. Did she somehow think that I was like Blanche, or that my life would be like Blanche's? No one could have mistaken me for someone glamorous like Blanche. I was at least as serious as my parents and twice as shy. Plus, there were those glasses thick as Coke bottles. However, I did gain the courage to sunbathe in our backyard after Blanche did it. And I started sneaking more cigarettes.

My mother also made another prophecy about my future. As an elementary school student, I wrote and illustrated many episodes of my story "The Adventures of Little Horse and Little Lamb," who were best friends, on my first grader's thick-lined paper. I also wrote a long and meandering story about a brother and sister, who were exactly like my brother and me, on a barefoot quest in the mountains of North Carolina, desperately searching for penicillin for a sick sibling. (I never made clear why they thought they'd find penicillin in the mountains, or why it was imperative for them to be barefoot; it may have had something to do with me reading *Tom Sawyer*). Mom, after seeing my work, told me that that she believed I would become a children's writer. I did exactly that. Was she prescient? Did I try to obey her? Looking back, I think that I will never know.

Dancing Holes in Her Shoes

The miseries of mining slate drove my father's ancestor, Owen Williams, from Caernarvon, Wales, to Lovingston, in the mountains of Virginia. I have heard the Williamses were discriminating people; during the winter they allowed the cow in the house but not the pig. My suspicion is that our family coped, not by leading strikes against mine-owners or freeing blind pit ponies, but by gathering around the fire in the stone cabin and seeing who could tell the best story.

My mother used to tell the story that when I was born, she took one look at my face and said, "That's Myrt!" She thought I looked exactly like my father's mother, Myrtle Williams, who I called Mommis Myrt. I admit to being chagrined, because I always admired my independent and feisty maternal grandmother more than the timid and retiring Mommis Myrt.

When she was visiting one year, Mommis Myrt confided in me that as a young girl at a barn dance she once danced holes in her shoes. That amazed me because as an old lady she seemed so reserved and shy. She was pretty much homebound because she never learned to drive. She left the house once a week on Thursdays, when a neighbor drove her to the grocery store and to get her hair done. The family story is that when my grandfather tried to teach her to drive, she drove the car straight into the carport post, was mortified, and never sat in the driver's seat again. She was a loving and generous person; Dad told me that when he was growing up one or more of his mother's relatives were always living with them.

Dad also told me that he briefly had a baby sister, but she died when she was about a week old. She was what they used to call a "blue baby," a baby with a heart defect. There was no crib for her; Mommis put her in the top drawer of a dresser to sleep. This story fascinated me as a child. I wandered around my grandmother's house, asking, "Is this the dresser where the blue baby slept?"

My grandfather died of a heart attack when Dad was sixteen, and Mommis Myrt lived with both sons after that, and then, after my mom and dad married, with my bachelor uncle, Reggie. She and Reggie used to spend most evenings rocking next to each other in the carport, chatting laconically. Mother and son both had a habit of shaking one foot while the other foot pushed against the ground, and they kept up a synchronous rhythm.

Reggie, one of our family's best storytellers, loved to tell tales about his mother. One of his funniest stories about Mommis Myrt involved her sly sense of humor. Once, the two of them went to Walmart in his two-seater Corvette, and on the spur of the moment decided to buy a new outdoor trash can. Back out in the parking lot, they realized that the trash can wouldn't fit in the Corvette. Mommis Myrt gamely agreed to ride home with the trash can over her head. Reggie recalled that drivers in other lanes looked at him pretty funny when they saw him talking to a trash can.

Another story Reggie told about Mommis Myrt was that once, a friend of his brought over a six-pack of beer when they were working together to assemble a grandfather clock. Reggie and his friend each drank one, leaving the other four in the refrigerator. Three months later, on a hot afternoon, Reggie drank another of the beers. Mommis declared, in a huff, "Reggie, looks to me like you've been hitting on that beer *mighty hard.*"

Mommis Myrt died young, at only sixty-nine. She'd had high blood pressure for many years, and her heart just gave out. I realize now, she'd had quite a bit of sorrow in her life, to lose a child and then her husband, and then to send two sons off to war.

After her funeral, thirty relatives stuffed themselves into her tiny lace-doily living room. I had loved her, and steeled myself for an anguishing afternoon. But conversation grew lively, the men standing to compete in storytelling (not the women, in those days, alas). Fortified by pound cake and coffee—my dad and Reggie were pretty much teetotalers but the progeny of Mommis's other siblings may have had additional fortification—the men went on for hours, until our sides hurt from laughing and tears ran down our cheeks. There were stories about Jesus and Arnold Palmer playing golf together, more stories about only God being able to hit a one-iron. It's a time I've remembered with joy for many years. I can just picture how my grandmother might have listened and laughed, her bony hands crossed over her stomach. She would have loved all that laughter in her honor.

Mommis Myrt, like me, was not a very inventive cook. Every time we ate at Mommis Myrt's house she fixed fried chicken, potato salad and succotash, with corn, lima beans, and tomatoes, my father's favorites. My grandmother's recipe for Welsh Christmas pudding, handed down through her family, takes two weeks to make. Even though she didn't enjoy cooking, she faithfully made it for us every year when we came to visit. That's love. And my half-Italian mother, the one who gave me the recipe, also made it many times to please my father and remind him of his family. That's love, too.

True confession: I did not like this pudding. It looked like a mottled boulder and I found it nearly inedible. However, if you're listening to a great story while eating it, you might not notice. Now, though, knowing the lengths my grandmother and mother went to in order to prepare this pudding for their families, I am in awe.

1 pound sugar
1 pound suet
1 pound bread crumbs
1 pound flour
1 box raisins
1 box currants
4 ounces citron
1 tablespoon orange peel, finely chopped
1 tablespoon lemon peel, finely chopped
2 teaspoons baking powder
Pinch of salt
4 eggs, beaten
1 tablespoon lemon extract
Enough milk to make stick together (about 1 cup)

In a large bowl, add the first 11 ingredients to the beaten eggs. Add the lemon extract. Add milk a little at a time and mix until ingredients are incorporated and stick together.

Tie the pudding in a wet cheesecloth that has been dredged in flour. Tie up, leaving a little room for the pudding to swell out.

Drop in boiling water and boil 4 hours in plenty of water. Then remove from water and without removing the cloth, place in a large bowl and shape into a flattened ball. Leave overnight.

The next day, remove from bowl but leave cloth in place. Allow to dry at room temperature for 10 to 15 days. Turn each day to dry all sides.

Serve with hard sauce made from sugar, butter, vanilla, eggs, and rum, brandy, or whiskey (though my grandmother refused to add the alcohol). Cut thin. Warm when you serve to soften the pudding.

Yield: 30 or more servings.

No, she wasn't outwardly independent or outspoken, qualities most people admire. But now I realize that Mommis Myrt was a truly loving soul, and I am proud to be from her family of storytellers. And yes, proud to be like her—why, I've danced holes in my shoes at least once myself.

Skipping MYF

I sat in the slippery wooden pew next to my brother, nervously shaking my foot. I was wearing pantyhose and heels and had used pink foam curlers the night before to curl my hair under. I wore lip gloss. I can't remember the dress I wore, but it's my guess that I wore a rust-colored flowered Villager dress that I had begged for because popular girls in my classes wore them. Beams of multi-colored light shone through the stained glass windows beside me, creating a beautiful pattern on the floor. My younger brother wanted to play tic-tac-toe on the back of a pledge envelope, but I was too nervous. Besides, he beat me at every game. I was going to have to walk up to the front of the church today and speak, so I motioned for him to put the pledge envelope back.

The other thirteen-year-olds in the Sunday school class and I were supposed to join the Methodist Church today. We'd been taking a class at Methodist Youth Fellowship for the past few months on Sunday evenings to learn the Methodist beliefs. We'd talked about eternal life, the teachings of the gospels, and becoming a disciple of Christ. I was very emotional about the fact that Jesus died for me. Every time I thought about it, I cried. I wanted to become a better person so that I would deserve it. Every time I sneaked a cigarette and blew the smoke out the bathroom window I thought maybe God could see me—as, of course, he could see all—and wondered if he'd forgive me.

MYF met on Sunday afternoons and early evenings in a little blue clapboard house next to the church. My friend Johnny and I often went out on the side porch to sneak smokes during free time. Johnny had sandy brown hair and blue eyes, and was somewhat overweight. He was obsessed with whether God would love him just the way he was. I wasn't a good person for him to ask about that, because I myself was hoping to change and improve to be worthy of God's love.

"God's love is unconditional," Johnny said, sitting on the edge of the porch and flicking his cigarette into the side yard.

"So you're saying He still loves us even though we're sneaking cigarettes?"

"Yes."

"He still loves us even though we're skipping MYF?"

"Yes."

"It just sounds too easy. It sounds like you can do anything you want and God will still love you."

"He will."

"So what's the motivation to be good?" I squinted at Johnny through the smoke, but he just gave me an enigmatic smile.

In spite of skipping class to smoke, though, I was emotional about my faith. I had seen my own father's piety, as he taught adult Sunday school every week before attending church. I realized that, even though I didn't seem capable of living the spotless life that might make my father and God proud, I still wanted them to be proud anyway. According to Johnny, God would still love me. But would Mom and Dad? I had my doubts.

Now, the preacher called Johnny's name, and he lumbered up

front and read his statement of belief, pushing his sandy bangs to the side with a self-conscious motion. He didn't appear nervous and did a good job with his reading. The MYF teachers were especially supportive of Johnny, since his parents didn't come to church and he rode with another family.

Since our last name was Williams, the last person to be called up by the minister was me. I stood with trembling knees, gripped my speech with shaky, cold fingers, and walked up front to the podium. I looked out on all of the dressed-up people sitting in the pews, gazing up at me expectantly. I was so frightened and overcome with emotion about this important day in my life that tears came to my eyes, and I drew a complete blank on what I had planned to say, even though I had practiced my speech many times at home. Reading my statement became impossible since my eyes were now completely blurred with tears. I tried roughly rubbing the tears away with the back of my wrist. My nose dripped onto my notes. I stumbled through my statement, swabbing my wet cheeks and sobbing by the end.

Once I finished, I continued to sob as my eight classmates and I repeated the Apostles' Creed together, in front of the church. Johnny gave me an encouraging look of understanding, and then the congregation stood and there was a responsive reading with the minister as the members welcomed us young people to the church and promised to care for us and guide us. The church members chanted that each of the young people were beloved children of their congregation, loved by God and perfect. I looked out in the audience and my mother looked very stern but as I repeated those words, I saw my father was crying too.

It was heartbreaking that Jesus had died for me and thought I was perfect and would forgive and love me even though I sneaked cigarettes and skipped MYF and there was even that time I let Howie pinch my nipple. And all the people in the church loved and forgave me too! I was overwhelmed with shame.

I was still weeping as I went back to rejoin my family. Usually my brother had ripped his fake clip-on tie from his shirt before heading out of church but today he was standing there staring at me with a pale, puzzled face, his tie still hanging there. I wonder if my show of emotion had in some way frightened him. My father, crying as hard as I was, put his arm around me and gently kissed my forehead. My mother, with a look of exasperation, laughed nervously, then dug into her black leather snap-clasp purse and jammed a wrinkled tissue into my hand.

"You should be ashamed of yourselves, both of you." That was the first time I realized that though Mom wanted us to be active in the church, she wasn't comfortable with public displays of emotion.

After joining the church, though our family still went to church, my participation in MYF fizzled. In high school, I made the drill team and became active in that and other activities.

Later in high school, I read a book called *The Chosen* by Chaim Potok that made a powerful impact on me and romanticized my view of religion and of Judaism. I believe my mother read it in her book club and gave it to me because she thought I'd enjoy it. I came away from this book knowing a bit more about Jewish culture and admiring the sacrifices that the characters made for their faith. This book created feelings in me similar to those I experienced that Sunday when I joined the church. As a teen, it seems I was susceptible to the emotions evoked by religious fervor, whether Christian or Jewish. Possibly this was the beginning of me finding room in my heart for the tenets of more than one religion.

Ornament Custody

The winter after my divorce from my first husband, I lived on cigarettes and chardonnay. One windy Saturday afternoon, three days before Christmas, I was at the kitchen table in Silver Spring, Maryland, in my flannel pajamas, cuddling my new cat, Cleo, when my friend Cheryl called me.

I pictured Cheryl in her bare kitchen. Also in her late twenties, recently divorced and without children, she was determined to save both herself and me. "I'm taking you to get a Christmas tree," she announced.

"Oh, no." Buying a Christmas tree, lugging it home, and decorating it felt like solving world hunger or climbing Everest. I blew a gray smoke cloud against the window and watched it billow back at me, relieved to be able to support my hometown, Winston-Salem, known as "cigarette city," even if I had failed at everything else.

"I'll be there in a half an hour," Cheryl said. "Be ready." Cheryl's father had been in the military. Inertia was not her friend.

By the time she arrived I had rejected several outfits based on the fact that they were either in the laundry, covered with cat hair, or too much trouble to put on. I had brushed Cleo's soft calico fur and lit another cigarette for further contemplation but that was all I had accomplished.

Cheryl's frosted hair was pulled into a severe career-woman's ponytail. A UCLA sweatshirt hung on her scarecrow-like frame. Her husband had left in May, mine in August. Neither of us had eaten a decent meal since. "Lisa! Get with it, girl! I am taking you to get a Christmas tree, dammit!"

Cleo laid back her translucent ears, leaped from my lap, and scrambled under the couch. Her yellow eyes followed Cheryl.

"Do you think he has a Christmas tree?" I wondered.

"Oh, for Crissake, if he does, who cares? You never loved him anyway." Cheryl, after forcing me to admit this terrible truth, then forced me into a pair of ill-fitting jeans and into the passenger seat of her Mazda RX-7. I hadn't been out of the house in a while and the frigid wind lashed tears to my eyes.

"Face it, Lisa, you yourself admitted you were still on the rebound from your college boyfriend when you settled for him. Well, you and I, we're not settling—ever again."

"Right," I said. People always asked us if we were sisters. This puzzled me. Cheryl is almost six feet tall, a veritable vortex of authority. I am barely five feet tall and routinely allow people to break in line in front of me. Our only similarities were the ubiquitous cigarettes and the frosted shade of our hair.

On the way to the tree lot Cheryl began one of her immensely entertaining stories. While never actually lying, she had a special gift for dramatic embellishment. "So anyway, after he left I was broke, he took everything. Until I got my first paycheck all I could afford was eggs. For two weeks, all I ate was eggs."

"Eggs? For two weeks?"

"Egg-zactly."

"Wow." Reid, too, had taken everything, mostly because I felt so very guilty for not loving him. I had shoved it all on him—cars, lamps, rugs, even the dog. He refused to take the house because he had recently refinanced it for more than it was worth.

Cheryl squealed into the tree lot and the Mazda lurched to a stop. I followed her over to the stand where the tree salesman in a gray hooded sweatshirt hovered over a space heater. "How much is your very best tree?"

The salesman pointed at a magnificent blue-green specimen. "Seventy-five dollars."

I grimaced. Then Cheryl spotted a waif-like bush that could have starred in a Charlie Brown special. It looked like a beaver had flossed with most of the branches on one side.

"You could put that side up against the wall," Cheryl whispered, then added loudly, "Most people already have their trees."

"You don't," the tree man pointed out.

"How much is it?" I asked.

"Twenty-five dollars."

Cheryl slapped her knee as if he had told the world's funniest joke. "That's the most pitiful-looking tree I've ever seen. Who would ever buy it?"

"You."

"We'll give you ten dollars for it."

The man chewed on his mustache and shrugged. "Okay."

"I don't even want a tree." This all seemed so very pointless. I longed to go back to my kitchen, smoke another cigarette, sink the tips of my fingers into Cleo's soft, soft fur, and pour cold chardonnay into a thin-stemmed glass. "I guess I can put that side up against the wall," I added, after Cheryl glared at me.

The hooded tree-man shouldered our Charlie Brown special, but when he saw the Mazda two-seater he blinked hard. "How do you plan to get this tree home?"

"Piece of cake. I'll take the top off and Lisa can hold the tree in her lap while I drive."

So I did. The wind chill must have been minus 100, and my skin crawled with being pricked by thousands of frozen green needles. The tree completely obliterated my view of the outside world and any view the outside world might have had of me. As far as anyone passing was concerned, Cheryl was out for a drive in dangerously cold weather with a tree.

A few hours later we agreed the tree didn't look so bad in my living room with the bald spot facing the wall. I climbed the attic stairs and retrieved the box of Christmas ornaments I'd been collecting for the past three or four years.

Reid liked saltwater aquariums, and one year I'd made a half-dozen tropical fish ornaments out of salt dough. I'd researched them thoroughly—I can still remember the queen angel and the yellow tang. My grandmother had crocheted and starched a box of white snowflakes. Friends and family had given me an eclectic combination of cat ornaments, and for the top I had a white peacock with a fantastical tail.

Cleo wiggled underneath the tree skirt, stalked the blinking lights, chewed the needles, and played soccer with a papier-mache cat. This was definitely the most fun she'd had since I'd adopted her.

Cheryl and I went to dinner after finishing the lights. She was in a hurry when she dropped me off because she had a date later. I thanked her for jolting me from my self-pitying stupor, and waved to her with a jauntiness I hadn't felt in months as she screeched around the corner. When I reached out to slide my key in the lock, I saw that the light was on in the living room and the door was slightly ajar. Someone was in my house.

With a quick intake of breath, I place my hand on the knob and slowly pushed the door inward. I stepped inside, and nearly collided with Reid on his way out, carrying a cardboard box.

"What are you doing here?" My heart heaved and I felt the tingle of racing adrenaline.

"I'm taking my half," he said. He wore an ancient argyle sweater of his father's I'd always disliked. His auburn hair was limp and unclean, his freckles were ghostly pale. He was so thin his Adam's apple looked like a knife edge, and there was a bloody piece of toilet paper stuck to it where he'd cut himself.

"Your half of what?" My voice was very loud, a combination of adrenaline and wine from dinner.

"The Christmas ornaments," he said. I focused on the box in his arms. Nestled in tissue paper were all of the fish ornaments.

"I made those!"

"You made them for me, they're mine," he shouted. "You loved me once!"

I glimpsed several of my grandmother's starched snowflakes. "You can't have my grandmother's snowflakes!"

"She told me I was a fine young man!"

I reached for the box, he tried to yank it from my reach, and slung the ornaments across the room.

There was a sort of snapping explosion in my head.

"Get out of here!" someone screamed, and Reid was backing

out the door because someone was punching and slapping him. The person had to be me, a fact my brain registered with faint surprise.

"I'm changing the locks!" I shouted as he sprinted down the block to where he'd parked his car. I slammed the door and leaned on it, then sank down to the floor. I had not loved him once, not ever, but I'd made everyone think I did, including myself. I crawled around the room picking up broken ornaments and wiping my face with the back of my hand.

Cleo ventured from under the couch. She sniffed the broken fish on the floor and rubbed up against my arm. She touched her nose to my wet,salty cheek, then licked it.

This I knew: My grandmother did not think Reid was a fine young man. She'd called him a "charmer," one of her pet words for no-good men, which also included "cad," "dandy," and "codger."

I glued the fish back together and while they dried on the kitchen counter I hung my grandmother's crocheted snowflakes on Charlie Brown's half-eaten branches. I plugged in the tree lights. They leaped to colorful brilliance, outlining a shape that was infinitely more perfect than the tree itself. When all the ornaments were hung I sat in the dark with Cleo on my lap, admiring the beauty imparted to that pitiful tree by all my work.

I felt I had made a breakthrough of sorts and ceremonially flushed the rest of my cigarettes down the toilet before going to bed. In the middle of a sensuous dream about my college boyfriend begging me to take him back I awoke to a loud crash.

Was Reid back? I sat upright, instantly alert, and remained still, listening. I heard only a faint tinkling noise. The digital clock glowed 4:22. I tiptoed to the landing and peeked into the living room below.

My tree was prone on the floor, a tangle of twisted lights, snapped branches, and rebroken ornaments. Cleo was crouched in the middle of it all, batting a broken fish-head with her soft white paw. She looked up at me and I swear she was smiling.

Wearily, I sat on the top step, my head clanging from too much wine. What difference would it make if I just left the mess until morning? Who cared, really, if I left it for a week? I ignored the sludge of defeat that had begun to ooze through my bones. With grim determination, I pulled Charlie Brown upright. Pine needles rained down and the water in the tree stand soaked the carpet. The lights were so tangled I had to take them off and start again. The fish ornaments had broken again, all in the same places. I reglued them. While waiting for them to dry I searched every drawer in the house, without success, for any cigarettes I might had missed in my zeal for reform. By sunrise I had restrung the lights, reglued and rehung the ornaments, and vacuumed.

The next night, Cleo, apparently pleased that I had restored her plaything to its previous state, climbed the tree again. Again I had it back up by dawn. Then I shoved her carrying case in the back seat for the seven-hour drive to my parents' house for Christmas. I stopped and picked up my grandmother in Richmond on the way, and put her old navy-blue suitcase on the back seat beside Cleo. Mom hates cats, and made Cleo stay in the basement, and whenever I went downstairs to visit her I sneaked one of the cigarettes I had bought at the gas station on the way down, while my grandmother was in the ladies' room.

Cheryl and I have both remarried and our kids go to camp together. We both quit smoking years ago. Our friendship has evolved into a sisterhood and I like to hope over the years I have helped her as much as she has helped me. I hear Reid has remarried and divorced again. My grandmother broke my heart when she died a month after I remarried. Cleo ran out in front of a car that very same week, which I prefer to think was purely coincidental. Cheryl is still gifted with a flair for dramatic storytelling; in her version of the story, I rendered Reid unconscious, and Cleo pulled down the tree for twelve nights in a row. Hearing this, our families roar with glee.

My husband is Jewish, but we have a prenuptial agreement that we will always have a Christmas tree. Most years, it's a joyous ritual. Sometimes it's a labor of grim determination. But I haven't missed a year.

Blizzard Babies

I had just delivered Caitlin, my first child, via C-section, and had been scheduled to take her home, but when I woke, the view from my hospital room revealed a white parking lot with snow so deep the cars were unidentifiable humps, like mattress batting.

"Lisa?" My husband Jeff called, his voice cracked with stress. "I'm going to try to dig the car out but I have no idea how long it will take."

"Oh, I can't stay another day!" I couldn't stand the antiseptic smells, the groans of pain, the cold floors, the endless waiting for someone to bring you something. Not to mention the nurses yelling at me for my maternal incompetence. I'd been stuck here for three days, waiting. Last night, my doctor had finally signed the release form. Now this.

"I'll try," Jeff said. "No guarantees."

I trundled dejectedly down the corridor, taking tiny steps to protect my incision. I wanted my own bed, my own shower, my own couch. I wanted to dress Caitlin in the little clothes I'd folded so neatly in the white dresser. Experienced mothers with older children had told me that the second time around, I'd invent ailments to stay longer. Maybe. Right now, I wanted to take my baby and go home.

I glanced into a room as I passed and saw a guy with an unsettling resemblance to my ex-husband. On the phone, standing next to a bed with a blond woman in it. He even had a similar insistent, cajoling tone to his voice.

"Lydia! You sound fabulous as usual, can you put me through to Jim?"

I took a good look. Good God, it WAS my ex-husband. I dashed past the doorway and out of his sight, instigating a searing pain suggesting I'd torn my incision, then leaned against the wall to catch my breath. I hadn't seen Reid in almost three years—with no children there had been no reason for contact—but I'd heard from mutual friends that he was still in the area and had remarried. A blast of emotion triggered simultaneous waterfalls of adrenaline, breast milk, and cold sweat.

What the hell was he doing here on the maternity ward? Did he have a new baby too?

Dazed, I limped to the nursery. A faint rhythmic throbbing had begun around my incision. I extended my wrist so the nurse could compare my bracelet to Caitlin's. Caitlin was asleep, her tiny nearly translucent fingers folded under her chin beneath the edge of the tightly swaddled blanket.

How was I going to get Caitlin back to my room without going back by Reid's?

I read the names printed on the ends of the bassinettes as I wheeled Caitlin by the bundled babies behind the picture window. Some lay in quiet wonder, some flailed, others were in varying stages of sleep. And there it was, "Byer," the last name that had been mine for four years. Inside was a long, thin, wailing baby.

Even at one day old, there was an resemblance. A baby that could have been mine but by a twist of fate, was not.

Okay, I would speed walk by his room, turning my face away so he wouldn't recognize me. Setting my jaw, I headed down the hall, one hand on the bassinette, the other pressed over my now-leaking incision. I glanced into the hospital room again as I passed and had no doubts. Reid, pacing rapidly, was still on the phone.

"Jim, buddy, I just want to stop in and show you some of the key man plans we can offer."

I shoved Caitlin's bassinette, like a cartful of groceries, into my room, skidded in, and slammed the door. I pressed my incision with my palm, which seemed to be the only thing right now to be preventing my intestines from spilling out onto the floor. I peered over the bassinette's edge. Caitlin's eyelids were purplish white, patterned with tiny pink veins.

I had dreamed about running into Reid. In those dreams I was slim and svelte, happy and published. Jeff, stunningly handsome, successful, witty and attentive, was at my side. In my more enjoyable dreams, Reid was toothless, and alone. He was always wearing the same awful red and gray argyle sweater.

I shuffled to the mirror. I still looked about four months pregnant. My stomach felt like semi-congealed Jell-O. My hair was thick from the pregnancy, but how careless of me to neglect washing and setting it during labor and delivery. I had on no makeup. My nightgown and robe didn't even match.

But it wasn't too late. Caitlin was still asleep. I turned on the shower and stripped down. Warm soothing water pummeled my aching, sagging body. Why should I be surprised to run into Reid in the hospital? After all, Reid was always in the hospital. For some reason, the moment Reid had said his vows, he had become an instant hypochondriac. The high-energy marketing major I'd married transformed overnight into a guy who would do almost anything to get admitted to whatever ward could squeeze him in. Double rooms were better because they provided built-in conversation victims, most of whom were in no shape to run out of the room. Once installed in a narrow bed with its matching narrow closet, Reid would put on a shapeless argyle sweater over his cotton gown and pad around the corridors discussing his ailments with anybody he happened to meet.

The last time had been five years ago when Reid had been hospitalized for a slipped disc. I had practically lived at the hospital, eating alone in the cafeteria, smoking in the courtyard, sitting beside Reid for hours, separated by only a white curtain from an enormous pale man who constantly tried to clear phlegm from his throat. That time, after Reid came home, during a short window of time in which he seemed healthy, I had left.

Now, thinking about Reid and his family two doors down, I felt my jaws involuntarily tighten. Not only had Reid taken our only good car, and the oriental rug my aunt had given us as a wedding gift, he was now keeping me prisoner in my hospital room with the door closed. And Jeff wasn't even here, whereas obviously Reid's new wife, having just given birth, was. He was definitely ahead. If you were keeping score. And, I realized, I was.

Smiling grimly, I rubbed blush on the taut muscles of my cheeks.

I had, with idiotic first-time mother optimism, brought a pair of pre-pregnancy black corduroys with me. The day after Caitlin was born I'd examined the waistband with hilarity and disbelief. Now I yanked them from my suitcase and tossed them onto the bed like a gauntlet, like a flag before a bull. Dammit, I was wearing those suckers. Just watch me.

I managed to pull the waistband up and over my rear end but with my leaking incision pulling up the zipper was out of the question. Fortunately, my maternity sweater now came down to my knees. The phone rang.

"Honey?" Jeff sounded as though he'd just run a 10k. "I've been trying for over an hour. I can't get the car out."

I looked out the window. Sparkling flakes swirled in a feverish dance. "Oh, please, Jeff, you can't leave me here."

"What's wrong? Is something wrong with Caitlin?"

I glanced at the baby. "What? No, no, she's fine, but this hospital's driving me crazy. I have to get out of here."

"Well, it's probably not even a good idea to transport the baby in this kind of weather."

I looked out the window at the glaring white. "Oh." A day by myself in the hospital hiding from Reid and his lovely wife, two doors down. I heaved what I knew was a very melodramatic and manipulative sigh. As usual, Jeff was being sensible.

"They're calling this the blizzard of the century. I'll keep trying but it doesn't look good."

Just as we hung up, Sandy, the nurse, bustled in. She plumped my pillows with karate chops. "Ready to try breast feeding again?"

"Okay." I picked up the baby as if she were porcelain, and glided, trying not to wake her, toward the bed. Sandy, with a disapproving glance, took Caitlin, dumped her on the bed, then unwrapped Caitlin's blanket and began to thump the bottoms of her feet.

"If she doesn't wake up to eat every four hours, you need to wake her up. Why don't you get in bed." It wasn't a question.

I complied.

"You need to time each side." Sandy twisted Caitlin's head and shoved it onto my breast as if she were handing off a football. Her hands looked red and worn, and she had no-nonsense lines around her mouth. "She's not made of glass."

"Uh-huh." This situation with Reid was so awkward. Surely the adult thing to do would be to congratulate him. Hiding out like this was ridiculous.

"You need to drink plenty of fluids." Sandy slid a tray with a cup of light green liquid within reach. "Otherwise you won't have enough milk. By the way, how's your incision? Let's have a look."

If Sandy saw it leaking she might not let me go home.

"It's fine. I just checked it."

Sandy narrowed her eyes, hesitated, then hurried out.

Breast feeding made me feel relaxed and sleepy. Caitlin had the most intoxicating smell. Just stroking her miraculously smooth and flawless cheek gave me the most exquisite feeling of well-being. I looked at the clock beside the TV and made a mental note to switch Caitlin to the other breast in ten minutes.

An hour or so later, I awoke with Caitlin fast asleep at my drained right breast while the left was so turgid it had begun to leak through my sweater. So had my incision. Painfully hoisting myself out of bed, I returned Caitlin to the bassinette.

I saw that Sandy had left the door open and crossed the room to close it.

At that moment Reid stepped into the hall.

Our eyes met for one of those fleeting instants before instinctive social graces kick in. Reid's face registered shock and embarrassment.

"Hi!" We both instantly stretched smiles across our faces.

"I heard from the Clarks that you were pregnant—" Reid gestured awkwardly at my abdomen.

"I thought I saw you this morning—"

We'd spoken simultaneously and now we both fell silent. Reid was thinner and less intimidating than I remembered.

"This is such an amazing coincidence." I smoothed my sweater to make sure it covered my unzipped pants. Maybe he wouldn't notice the large yellow stain clinging to my left breast at the top of the sweater and the smaller pink one bunched down below. "I have a baby girl. What about you?"

"A boy," Reid said. "He sure is something. Laura's feeding him now. Listen, why don't I bring them over? Laura would love to meet you."

How very civilized. Behind me, in the room, the baby fussed a little. Warm colostrum spurted out of my swollen left breast.

"Sounds perfect," I said. "Give me about ten minutes, okay?"

I skidded into the bathroom and tried to pump my milk into a baby bottle. I gave up after spraying milk on the mirror, the wall, the toilet, and into my own eye. There seemed to be no way of telling which way the milk was going. Finally I squirted it into the sink. I know the nurse would yell at me, but Caitlin was deeply asleep and what the hell else was I going to do? I'd just finished stuffing a folded piece of toilet paper over the soaked incision bandage when my visitors arrived.

"Hi." Laura, pushing her baby's bassinette, had blond, curly hair, jingly silver earrings, and wore a man's plaid robe. She looked a little like Reid's mother might have looked decades ago. "What a coincidence, hey? I've always wanted to meet you. I bet you and Reid set this up." She laughed.

"Come on in," I said. "What's his name?" The baby's face was still red, and to me, he looked and smelled very unappealing.

"Reid Junior," Reid boomed. "What else?" I had forgotten how loud Reid's voice was.

"Isn't he a pistol? Let's take a look at your little stinker." Reid and Laura peered over the edge of the bassinette as Caitlin slept.

"How sweet," said Laura.

I gazed with awe at the curve of Caitlin's lashes as they brushed her cheeks, her flawless skin, and the downy hair on the nape of her neck. Her aroma was an absolute aphrodisiac. She was not, excuse me, a stinker.

"How much weight did you gain?" Laura settled herself beside Reid on my bed.

Rather a personal question, I thought, for someone I'd known for less than five minutes. I lowered myself onto the nursing chair and shifted my weight to one thigh. With both a C-section and an episiotomy, any position was a challenge.

"Laura gained twenty pounds exactly, and she's already lost all but three pounds," Reid shouted before I could answer. "Doesn't she look great?"

"Oh, yes." So he was keeping score, too.

"We went all natural," Laura announced. "How about you?"

"Oh, the cord was around Caitlin's neck so I had to have a C-section."

"Too bad."

Two points to the plaid team.

"Well, at least her head doesn't look smushed," I said, wincing at my own audacity. Two for the unzipped corduroy team.

Sandy popped in and with rapid sleight of hand replaced my empty juice cup with a full one and placed a little paper cup containing a pain pill on my tray.

"Laura's labor was eighteen hours and she never took a thing. A couple of times she was begging for it but she made me promise not to let her have anything so I didn't." Reid squeezed his wife's shoulder with exaggerated affection.

Three pointer.

"Did you know we videotaped Reid Junior's birth?" Laura said.

"I was right down there with the camera in closeup living color," Reid chimed in. "Even when Laura was in transition and she was screaming her fool head off."

"Goodness," I said, having completely lost track of the score.

"Listen," said Reid suddenly. "I hold no grudge whatsoever, do you, Lisa?"

Well, except for the car, Aunt Katherine's oriental rug, and four years of my life. But I smiled. "Of course not."

"Everything was for the best," Reid boomed, squeezing his wife's shoulder again. "Although I want you to know, Lisa, that I did have to go back to the hospital and get my back operated on after all, and recuperation was no picnic."

Laura rolled her eyes. I smiled and nodded, feeling a sudden affection for her.

"I see you're still wearing that lovely argyle sweater," I said to

Reid. Briefly, remembering him plodding down the hospital halls in this shapeless sweater, a lump formed in my throat. I knew, now, why he kept getting sick while we were married, and I was glad he'd found someone to love him.

I wish Jeff had walked in at just that moment, his black hair sparkling with melting snow, his cheeks beet red from the cold, having hailed a passing snowplow. Maybe Jeff would have proved himself to be much the better match for me, and Reid would have shown himself to be happy with Laura. And Jeff would have braved the elements to take me home from the hospital just the way I wanted.

But instead, Laura said, "Maybe we'll run into each other in nursery school orientation," then pushed her baby's bassinette out the door. As she passed, I looked down at the baby again. His eyes moved back and forth under his closed translucent lids, and I wondered what he was watching in there, and decided he seemed quite lovable after all. Then Reid and his family were gone.

Jeff didn't make it to get Caitlin and me until the next day. It turned out that my brother-in-law was also stuck in the hospital, as the snow had hit while he was visiting his father, who was very ill, and he stopped by and took some videos of Caitlin that are nothing less than priceless. He took one particular shot of me holding her close where I'm puckering up trying to kiss her and she is imitating me, squinting and puckering, too. We both have the most unbelievably chapped lips; we look as though we've been through a battle together, and in a way, we have. Our lips are so chapped we look as though we'd slice each other open with the slightest kiss.

"You wouldn't believe the coincidence," I said to Jeff when he finally arrived. "My ex-husband Reid and his wife Laura are two doors down. She just had a little boy. Do you want to meet them?"

"No," said Jeff, who has always avoided small talk. He wasn't the least bit jealous of my ex-husband and had no desire to revisit the past. He has always looked forward. "We need to get out of here. It's supposed to start snowing again. Ready?"

"Yes. We just need to put on Caitlin's snowsuit."

Her bowed spindly legs reached only an inch or so below the crotch, leaving the entire lower section of the snowsuit dangling empty. Her little hands barely reached the suit's armpits. Jeff leaned over her, his face fatigued, but with an expression of such tenderness that my eyes stung and my throat felt tight.

Sandy, pushing a wheelchair, patted the seat, indicating I was to sit down. "Hospital rules." I sat. "Now, Dad, why don't you let Mom carry the baby."

Jeff was Dad. I was Mom. Jeff reverently laid Caitlin in my lap.

Sandy bent to rearrange Caitlin's blankets, her red, lined hands in sharp contrast to Caitlin's ivory skin. I slid my finger under Caitlin's tiny hand and with a pure and magical reflex, Caitlin's fingers circled mine. The trusting way she slept as I held her told me that the games were over. This was a whole new world.

Writing Test

"We're not allowed to mention time," the teacher says as I follow her into the copy center that will serve as today's testing room. "He gets as much time as he wants."

J.T. is small for his age, with smooth, babyish cheeks and child-like hands. His too-tight shirt is faded with repeated washings, and his jeans pool around his ankles. Constantly, he taps the heel of one untied basketball shoe on the floor. He plays with his pencil, drops it repeatedly, bends to pick it up, then finds a tape dispenser and sticks small pieces of tape on the table and onto his pants, and after that he grabs a phone book and accordions through it, then drops his pencil again. Picks it up.

"Okay, J.T.," the teacher says, as she takes the phone book from him. "You need to listen to these instructions. I am only allowed to repeat them once."

All seventh grade public school students in North Carolina must take this writing test. My job as proctor is not only to make sure the students don't cheat, but also to make sure the teachers don't give in to the temptation to help them.

Normally, when I proctor, I patrol a classroom while the teacher reads instructions such as "Do not open your test booklet until I say to do so. You will have ninety minutes to complete this portion of the test. You may begin." Twenty-five students then scribble their outlines or create their bubble maps and then the room is filled with the fevered scratching of twenty-five pencils as they regurgitate five-paragraph essays. Today, however, I'm proctoring only one student—J.T., who receives special testing conditions.

I'm a writer, on deadline, but I seem to be blocked, so when the secretary called and said they were desperate, I came.

The teacher begins to read the instructions. J.T. wants to keep his own green pencil, but it's not a Number Two, and the teacher says he must use one the school provides. He picks up a school pencil, but when the teacher looks away, he exchanges it for the green one, glancing at me to see if I notice.

Should I say something? Maybe the computer won't be able to read his answers and his test will be thrown out.

"He's using his own pencil." I feel like a snitch.

After a minor skirmish, J.T. relinquishes his green pencil. The teacher finishes reading the instructions. The prompt is something about students being tardy too often.

"J.T., do you have any questions?"

J.T. stares at the ceiling. "No."

"You may begin."

The teacher starts grading papers. I watch the second hand inch around my watch face. J.T. continues to stare at the ceiling. He drops the pencil. When he picks it up, he tries to shove it into the side panel of the desk. He twirls it in his hands, examining with great care the eraser and the strip of metal attaching the eraser to the pencil. Perhaps he wonders what makes it superior to his own. He leans back and stares at the ceiling.

I wonder if J.T. remembers that he's supposed to be taking a test.

I pick up a geography textbook from a box next to my chair. I examine a map showing Utopian communities in the U.S. during the 1840s.

J.T. leans his head back, way back, and examines the ceiling tiles. His eyes travel to the far corners of the room.

I study the cluster of Utopian communities in the northeast, as well as a few in the upper Midwest. There don't appear to have been any here in the South.

Minutes pass. And more. I could be here all day. Not that it matters, since I am stuck in my writing, somehow, anyway. But we're not allowed to mention time.

"J.T., do you need me to read the instructions again?" the teacher asks. "I'm allowed to read them to you once more."

"No," J.T. says.

"Okay." The teacher nods and smiles encouragingly. "I know you can do this, J.T. I have complete confidence you can do it."

I lack that confidence. I picture J.T., the teacher, and myself, like Rip Van Winkle, trapped in this room, growing gray-haired and shriveled, as civilizations rise and fall around us.

I get an idea. What about mental telepathy? I once read a story by Isabel Allende in which a small girl uses telekinesis to make an ash tray move across a coffee table. If I focus in the same manner, maybe I could get J.T.'s pencil to move across the page, producing words. I outline J.T.'s essay in my mind and concentrate, trying to transmit each sentence one at a time. I know this is absurd, yet I knit my brow, willing J.T. to pick up the pencil and write something, anything. The minutes tick by.

I am a writer and if I were in a room such as this one with two people watching my every move I couldn't write a word either. I can't write a word anyway.

How important is it, in the overall scheme of life, for J.T. to do this? When will he ever need to write a five-paragraph essay? With technology, when will he ever need to write anything? I imagine him in ten years. Maybe after the water pipes in his house burst one winter, and he needs to fill out insurance forms, he will need to write a description of the items he has lost. If he witnesses a crime, or commits one, he will need to write a statement describing what happened. Maybe once in his life he will want to write a love letter. "These are the three reasons I love you."

Thirty-seven minutes have elapsed. J.T. hasn't touched either his answer sheet or the scratch paper he is to use to write his outline.

I put away the geography book to focus more intensely on my telepathic efforts to help J.T. I scrunch my eyes together, almost put both hands to my temples like Mr. Spock when he did the Vulcan Mind Meld. *Write!* I practically shout inside my head.

Now J.T. has begun tearing small pieces of tape from the dispenser and placing them in a column on the left side of his answer sheet. What is he doing? He carefully lines these all the way to the bottom of the sheet. Finally I tap the teacher's arm.

"No, J.T., your answer sheet won't go through the computer."

"But I'm doing it to help me indent."

Indent? Then he is actually considering writing? I feel something akin to joy. Being careful not to tear his answer sheet, the teacher and I help J.T. remove the pieces of tape.

J.T. picks up the Number Two pencil.

"I think," he writes.

It happens so fast that if I blinked I would have missed it. J.T. has been thinking! "I think, therefore I am." College philosophy – Descartes, was that right? I feel light-headed with success, anticipating what the next moments will bring. *I think, therefore I am.* And I have an epiphany: Writing this essay *is* important. J.T. himself has blasted a ragged sky-blue hole in my cynicism.

But now time slows to a crawl again. J.T. places his hand on the instruction sheet and slowly runs his finger across the page, moving his lips as he reads the instructions to himself.

"Can you help me?" he asks the teacher.

"No, I'm sorry, J.T., I'm not allowed to."

J.T. nods with sad acceptance, then tries again. "What about spelling?"

"Mrs. Kline and I are not allowed to help you in any way."

That doesn't count our secret weapon, does it, J.T.? Our Vulcan Mind Meld? Write, now, write. Tardiness is unrelated to godliness. In a Utopian community, no one is ever tardy. In Utopian communities, people learn with ease, and they write with ease. They are not forced to endure the humiliation of writing a five-paragraph essay while two people watch like vultures. And what they think and what they write matters. My brain sizzles with the effort, but I don't give up because *I know it is working.* J.T. has written, "I think."

J.T. picks up his pencil. He scoots his chair closer to the table. He hunches over the test paper and then magically, miraculously, words begin to spill from his Number Two pencil like oil from a well. He doesn't stop at the ends of sentences, he merely jabs a period onto the paper and rushes on.

I am praying, write five paragraphs, write your introduction, your three reasons why, and your concluding paragraph. Use active verbs. Descriptive adjectives. I watch in stunned fascination as this boy, in whom I had no faith, somehow manages to reach down inside himself and excrete the words drop by drop, as if they were his own blood. Like a weapon, he grips the Number Two pencil, until his fingertips turn a bloodless white. Tears come to my eyes.

"I'm finished," he says.

"Are you sure?" the teacher asks.

"Yes." He drops his pencil and slumps back in his chair, repeatedly opening and closing his fingers like a video game champ.

"Then you may close your test booklet. You have completed the writing test."

She gives me J.T.'s answer sheet to return to the guidance counselors. As she steps outside with me, she tells J.T. he may get out a Scrabble board until the test period is over. He has finished thirty minutes early.

"I love Scrabble!" J.T. shouts. With a burst of joyous energy, he runs to the cabinet and pulls out the worn and flattened box.

We read his ten line essay together, the teacher and I. I know his fate but ask her anyway. "Will he pass?"

"No," says the teacher. "It has to be five paragraphs. But it doesn't matter." She tells me that after the test booklets were printed the state office discovered a problem with the prompt. The tests will be graded, but none of the tests in any of the schools will count this year. "We told the other kids," she says, "but with kids like J.T., well, it's almost too hard to explain."

I take J.T.'s test booklet and Number Two pencil to the guidance office.

After that, inspired by J.T., I go home to write.

Eleanor Hill

I adored my grandmother, Eleanor Hill Verra. We used to visit her in Richmond, Virginia, at her row house on Mulberry Street. I loved the narrow, twisting stairs in her house, the antique china angels she lined on the mantelpiece every Christmas, the lace doilies on the arms of her easy chairs, the "fizzes" she made with ice cream and ginger ale, and the way she treated any scrapes or boo-boos with vinegar and soda. I loved to walk over and feed the ducks at Byrd Park, not far from her house. Every Easter, for several years, when my brother and I were little, she gave us baby chicks, ducklings, or bunnies, much to our delight and our parents' chagrin.

Eleanor, born in 1895, grew up in a tiny town called Atlantic on the coast of North Carolina. There were no roads to get there at first; the only way to get there was by boat. The mailboat came once a week. Her father was a fisherman, and she was the youngest of ten children. Her mother, who loved to read, often read aloud in the afternoons to children of the Atlantic community. She died in childbirth when Eleanor was two. As a teen, Eleanor left home to live with a cousin in New Bern, where she went to school and found a job at a car dealership. Because she worked at the dealership, she learned to drive, and was one of the first women in New Bern to do so. She also lived through the 1918 flu epidemic in her twenties, which makes more of an impression on me now than it did before, since we've been living through Covid. Eventually she moved to Richmond, Virginia, to go to beauty school, and met and married my grandfather, Americus, affectionately called "A.E.," who was a handsome and charming Italian widower. He wrote her flowery love letters, calling her such things as "a paragon of womanhood" while they were courting. As a newlywed, my grandmother lived with her husband A.E., his blind mother, and his rebellious preteen daughter, Blanche. My mom was their only child together, and A.E. died of a heart attack when Mom was seven. By that time, the mother-in-law had passed away and Blanche had married Maurice Salomonsky and moved out of the house. After that, my grandmother supported herself and my mother by turning her home into a boarding house, restoring hats, and also making costumes at the Mosque, a Richmond theater. She was a creative person, a maker of things, and she had taught herself how to sew, embroider, crewel, cross-stitch, and knit. As a single mother, she managed to hang onto her house through the depression as well as send her daughter to college after World War II.

As a toddler, I tried to say "Grandmother Verra" and it came out as "Mommis Verra," and that stuck and everyone in our family called her that from then on. Mommis came to visit us quite often, and she stayed in my bedroom. When I was a child, she would tickle my back as I fell asleep at night. While Mommis and I had a loving relationship of mutual adoration, she and my mom had a volatile one. I have such vivid memories of them fighting in the kitchen.

"I'm going to fix these beans," Mommis would say, tying an apron around her waist.

"No, Mother, I can fix them, you don't need to do that. Go sit down." Mom waved at her to go back out into the family room.

"I want to earn my keep! I am not going to sit down while you wear yourself to a frazzle. I'm going to fix these beans!"

"Mother, for the love of Mike, go sit down!"

I did not know who Mike was but it was an expression my parents used fairly often. And I really was baffled by the importance of who fixed the beans (which both of them fixed in the traditional southern way of boiling them all afternoon until the nutrients all ended up in the water). Possibly my grandmother was simply trying to help, and my mother interpreted her offers as attempts to take over. Both were strong-willed women, and it seemed to me that their relationship was always a battle of wills. My grandmother had opposed Mom marrying my father because she thought he was too poor. Little did she know how ambitious and smart my dad was. Now I wonder if the true subject of the fights about the beans was Dad. Anyway, after fights like that, I would come home from school the next day and my grandmother would be gone. She had packed her little blue suitcase and taken the bus home. She always left a twenty dollar bill on top of our TV. I was heartbroken.

I wrote my first novel, *Eleanor Hill*, about her. After she died, my mother gave me all her letters and photographs. She had saved boxes and boxes of them, all the way back to when she was a teen. I couldn't look at them at first, but after a few months I started going through them, and was fascinated. One of the oldest letters was from 1909, when a boy wrote her a note asking if he could walk her to church that Wednesday. *Eleanor Hill* is a fictionalized story, based on her letters and photos, about her young adulthood in Atlantic and New Bern around 1910. While she lived a fairly ordinary, sometimes lonely life, I felt that she was an independent and resourceful woman for her time, and that hers was a life worth remembering and memorializing. When I finished writing *Eleanor Hill*, in 1998, thirteen years after she died, I sent it to two small publishing companies. In those days, many children's publishers accepted manuscripts without an agent. Both publishing companies offered me a contract. I was elated and stunned. *Eleanor Hill* won the North Carolina Juvenile Literature Award when it came out. Years later, when *Eleanor Hill* went out of print, a dear friend who has a small publishing company offered to reprint it. I was so honored and touched. My multi-talented daughter, Kelsey, designed the beautiful new cover.

My grandmother died just two months after I married Jeff. The irony is that she died on my parents' anniversary, and that the only person with her was my dad, the son-in-law she had opposed, as my mom had run out to the store.

I felt her presence in the nursery after I had Caitlin, whose middle name is Eleanor. I truly felt her there, gazing into the crib at her great-granddaughter and namesake. I also felt her presence at my desk as I wrote *Eleanor Hill*. And I still feel her presence with the pillows, curtains, embroidery, ponchos, winter scarves and hats, and wall hangings, all of the things that she made that still surround me with her love.

A Contrast of Courtships and Faiths

Religion was a large part of my parents' young lives. They met at a Methodist Youth Fellowship meeting in the 1940s. Both of them were officers in MYF at their respective churches. Mom attended the Boulevard Methodist Church in downtown Richmond, Virginia, and Dad attended the one on Patterson Avenue in the suburbs.

My grandmother told me that on that day, Mom had to make a presentation to the other church youth, and she chose to wear a gray dress.

"Mitzi, why are you wearing such a plain dress?" my grandmother asked.

"I don't want them to pay attention to how I look," my mother apparently responded. "I want them to pay attention to what I say."

Gray dress or not, Mom was a dark-haired beauty with a streak of independence and my dad did indeed notice her that day. As Dad told it, after the meeting he went home and told his mother he'd met the girl he was going to marry.

According to Mom, that was sometime in the fall. A mere seven months later, Dad called Mom and invited her to go to the Easter sunrise service with him.

Mom loved telling the story of their first date. "First of all," she'd say, "he told me he'd been trying to get in touch with me. Seven months! He waited seven months to ask me out! Just how hard was he trying, I'd like to know? And second of all, to invite *me* to get up at five o'clock in the morning to go somewhere?" Our family always laughed at this, as Mom was notoriously not a morning person. On Saturdays she often didn't get up until noon, worn out from her week of teaching. Nearly every Sunday, because of our mother, we were late to the eleven o'clock church service. "I turned him down flat!" my mother would say with an exasperated laugh. "Then, a few hours later, I felt guilty and called him back and agreed to go."

"She was just playing hard to get," Dad would say with a wink and a laugh. As an adult, I realized Dad had no money for courting. The Easter sunrise service was, of course, free. He'd grown up in a straitlaced Methodist family where his social life revolved around the church. I imagine it was the only place he could think of to take the girl he felt so passionate about, and apparently knew he was going to marry.

After that first date, their courtship lasted seven years, through World War II and after my dad came back and finished school on the GI Bill. They finally married in 1952. Their first month of marriage, they invited another couple over to play cards and they served popcorn and Cokes. "That was our entertainment budget for the month," my father told me with a grin.

Dad was a physicist. There are lots of scientists, of course, who don't believe in God, but I believe that Dad's knowledge of the immutable laws of physics actually reinforced his belief in God and convinced him further of the magnificent genius of the creation of the universe. How could the laws of physics be so ironclad and so miraculous if there was no God? Jewish atheist Albert Einstein once said, "There are only two ways to live your life. One is as if nothing is a miracle. The other is as if everything is a miracle." My dad was a scientist who chose the second way. One of my dad's favorite Bible quotations was, "Whosoever believeth in Him shall not perish but shall have life everlasting." He believed in the Apostles' Creed. He believed in everlasting life. He taught Sunday school for thirty years. He tithed for his entire life. He prayed regularly and cried when he sang hymns. He was a true believer. And while he was too old for the bracelets that said, WWJD? ("What would Jesus do?") that was the perfect essence of the way he lived his life.

Jeff's grandfather, Nathan Zagoria, came over from a small town called Preile, in Lithuania, in about 1915. The family story is that in his shtetl, the Russians were recruiting Jewish boys to march in the front lines as soldiers. It was a death sentence. Nathan's parents, who had seven sons, sent their eldest son Nathan, who was about eighteen, and his younger brother, Max, to America, hidden in the engine room of a cargo ship. They paid a man to bring food to the engine room for the boys, but the man apparently took the money and spent it on liquor, and didn't bring the boys anything. After the boys had been hidden in the engine room for a few days, licking condensation from the pipes to survive, Nathan used his shoelace to write a note on a scrap of paper asking for food. When a crew member came into the engine room, he dropped the note down to him. The sailor picked up the note, looked at it, and threw it down and left the engine room. Nathan soon realized the sailor couldn't read. Or at least couldn't read his language. Nathan tried again with another crew member, and was in luck. The man read the note, and brought the two boys some grapefruit juice. He also helped smuggle the boys off the ship when it docked, and that night a woman allowed the boys to sleep on the floor of her shop, and gave them some money for the train to New Jersey, where their uncle was a fruit vendor and would give them jobs.

But in the train station, every time a train would stop they would not get on. All the seats in the trains were red, and Nathan and Max knew that in Russia, red meant first class, and they couldn't afford that. Finally a man who had been watching them and listening to them talk came over and said, "Why don't you get on the train?" When Nathan explained about the red seats, the man laughed and said, "In America, all the seats are red. Get on the train!" So the boys did, and they made it to New Jersey.

Eventually the boys learned from their uncle how to become fruit vendors, and that was the way Jeff's grandfather earned his living throughout his life. He grew his business, had an arranged marriage to a Jewish girl who worked as a seamstress in a New York sweatshop, and he also became president of a small synagogue. Jeff's family describes his grandfather as "dynamic." He was beloved in the family. Judaism was his full identity. He probably never even knew many people who weren't Jewish, except possibly some of his fruit customers. Jeff revered his grandfather; when Jeff was in college and vet school he visited him in the Hebrew Home in Bethesda nearly every day when he was in town.

Eventually, all of Nathan's brothers came to America, and now their progeny live all over the country, from New York to California to Florida. The family has, by and large, amalgamated into American culture and society. Most family members are Conservative or Reformed rather than Orthodox, there has been some intermarrying, and some grandchildren have been raised Christian. Some, like Jeff's aunt and uncle, attend the Unitarian Church, though they still identify as Jewish.

While I never got to know Jeff's father's family as well, I think of them as being more religious. Some are Orthodox, but most are Conservative. None that I know of have married non-Jews. Jeff's father attended the minyan, or the quorum of ten men required for worship, at synagogue every day of his life.

Jeff's father and mother knew each other as high school students in Somerville, New Jersey. The story that Jeff's mother tells is that Ira was very good-looking and was chased by quite a few other girls, but she was proud of the fact that she got him. Photos of her as a young woman show she also was strikingly beautiful and vivacious. When Ira was drafted into the army, he and Etta went to her father.

"Pop," Etta said, "Ira and I have decided we're going to get engaged, and we'll get married when Ira gets back."

"Engaged, shmengaged," said Nathan. "Eh! You'll get married."

So they did. Ira left for the war soon after, and Etta continued to live with her parents. While Ira was in Europe fighting, Etta came down with appendicitis and had to be hospitalized to have her appendix removed. Once Ira returned, Nathan apologized to his son-in-law.

"I feel like I'm giving you damaged goods," he said. The truth was that he knew Ira couldn't afford the hospital bill, and paid it himself.

Jeff's mother loves telling this story, and she tells it with good humor. She is completely aware of the misogynistic message it sends, hearkening back to the days when fathers paid men to take their supposedly useless daughters off their hands. But Jeff's mother never worried at all about the agonies of history that often torment and paralyze me; she has always lived life with zest and good humor and has never hesitated to exert the sheer power of her personality whenever necessary, whether with her husband, her son, her daughter, or her grandchildren.

Jeff tells stories about Nathan's children and grandchildren meeting at the beach for the Passover Seder every spring, and sitting at a long table with Nathan at the head, leading the Seder and "davening," or praying. Meanwhile, side conversations and gossip were going on all along the table and everyone would be having their required cups of wine and Nathan would offer his opinions on the side conversations and gossip in between prayers.

Because getting into veterinary school in the United States was so difficult when Jeff applied, he went to veterinary school in the Philippines. During his second year Jeff was stressed and challenged. There was martial law in the Philippines at the time. Because of the cost, Jeff was only able to talk on the phone with his parents about once a month.

"There are guys with machine guns on every corner," Jeff said. "The teachers expect us to memorize and recite the textbooks."

"And, honey, there's a typhoon expected to hit there," his mother added.

"I'm watching cows float down the street in front of my house right now, Ma," he said. "I want to come home. I'll try to get in graduate school in the States."

"Things sound very difficult," his father agreed.

"You come home," his mother said.

But then they told his grandfather about the conversation. His grandfather, who had licked the condensation from engine pipes to make it to America.

His grandfather said, "Eh, he stays." And he did.

Jeff always says he wishes I could have met his grandfather, because he was such a dynamic person. I wish I could have.

"Do you think he would have liked me?" I've asked, so many times, often over anniversary dinners when we tend to reminisce.

"He would have loved you," Jeff assures me.

"Would he have approved of me, even though I'm not Jewish?"

"He would have loved you," Jeff says again.

That warms my heart.

In spite of the religious and cultural differences, Jeff's and my families were very similar. We both came from academic families. My father had a PhD and so did Jeff's. And eventually, so did my mom. Both fathers had earned their education via the GI Bill. Our family cultures both prioritized education, hard work and achievement. Dad taught physics at Wake Forest and Jeff's father worked at the National Institutes of Health. Our economic backgrounds were similar as well—I saw a picture of Jeff as a baby on their small screened porch and it looked almost identical to a picture of me as a baby on my parents' back porch. His family home was in Maryland and mine was in North Carolina, but honestly, they could have been next door. The only obvious difference between our families, on the surface, was that one celebrated Christmas and Easter and the other celebrated the High Holidays, Hanukkah, and Passover. Both of our fathers were devout, while our mothers had a more social, cultural understanding of religion.

I don't believe that marrying a person of a different religion was something that either Jeff's parents or mine would have ever been able to do. On both sides, their religion was too important to their identity. Both Jeff and I are very grateful for our parents' open-minded and accepting approach to our union.

Finding Hanukkah Wrapping Paper:
Notes on an Interfaith Marriage

One of my mother's teacher friends had a Jewish husband, Ron, who was known for his matchmaking skills (six couples he'd introduced had married). I had been divorced and single for about a year, living in Silver Spring, Maryland, sharing a house with a friend, when I met Ron through my mom.

"I have a cousin who lives near you and I think you'd get along," Ron said. I had been dating a guy from work who spent several hours of every date trying to impress me with his guitar skills, which were singularly awful. I was open to meeting someone new.

Jeff claims that I turned him down the first few times he asked me out, which is true, because, polite Southern girl that I am, I was having trouble getting rid of the guitarist. Finally Jeff and I went out on a Friday night. I think his mother suggested the restaurant—it was called Nova Europa. An old-world type of place, it featured low lighting, lots of candles, white tablecloths, heavy dishes such as braised veal and beef bourguignonne, and red leather banquettes. We ended up talking until past ten o'clock. I thought Jeff was incredibly attractive—dark-haired and slim, high-energy to the point of being almost frenetic. He has since told me that he found my ankles very sexy, which of course I could have a number of responses to, but won't. He was a veterinarian, which attracted me, because I love animals (I had a beloved cat as a child that I had to sneak in the house through my bedroom window) and I had a feeling that anyone who would become a veterinarian was a compassionate person. Jeff very much is. He's definitely the nurse and caretaker in our family. He was also a guitarist (a good one) and an athlete. Our second date was to a basketball game. I can't remember who was playing or who won. What I remember is that my contact fell out and, miraculously, Jeff found it. What a hero! And our third date was to crack crabs (we were in Maryland, after all) at a Silver Spring place called The Crab Shack, and we stayed so long, telling each other the stories of our lives, that the staff hung around rolling their eyes and staring at the ceiling, waiting for us to leave. Jeff had gone to veterinary school in the Philippines and I was fascinated by his stories of his life there. We went straight to his place and hopped into bed after that. The girl he had been dating kept calling and he kept hanging up on her. We couldn't keep our hands off each other.

Jeff's first marriage had lasted only four months. I believe Jeff's family was more receptive to me because of that first failed marriage to the requisite Jewish girl. After the mess of such a quick divorce, I think they were eager for him to be happy. And our families sort of knew each other, since Mom taught high school with Ron's wife. Also, fortunately, there had been more than one interfaith marriage in the family already. Jeff's older sister's husband had been Christian and converted to Judaism before they wed. And Ron's wife Kat was, like me, a Christian. I don't know if Ron converted to Christianity or not, but he did sometimes attend the Methodist Church with Kat. Our interfaith marriage was not fraught with family disapproval, banishment, or lack of forgiveness, as so many have been. My family welcomed Jeff with open arms and his family welcomed me. We were so lucky.

My friends have told me that the early stages of Jeff's and my relationship were a bit sickening to watch because we were so wrapped up in each other. We wanted to be together every minute and there was no room in our world for anyone else. We'd get invited to parties and then leave early so we could be alone. In some ways I regret that, because I worry that kind of infatuation is essentially selfish, but I also feel blessed to have had that kind of all-consuming experience, because not everyone does.

One day Jeff and I were on a run together and, huffing and puffing, Jeff said, "I think we should get married."

I ran a few more steps, then stopped and looked at him. I was expecting the question—in fact, I had known since about that third date that he would ask me—and I also knew that I would say yes. But still I told him I had to think about it. Maybe I wanted to be more careful because of my first mistake. For whatever reason, I told him yes after about two days, during which I really wasn't thinking at all, because I had already made up my mind.

At that point, he told me that he'd talked to his parents about it and they had not insisted that I convert, but only asked if we could raise our children Jewish. I would have agreed to anything. So I said okay. Children were so far in the future, amorphous and distant. Looking back, I realize I should have thought about it in a deeper way, and Jeff and I should have discussed our individual religious beliefs more thoroughly at this point, but we didn't. I regret that.

We decided to get married on the first of June, on a Saturday night. I learned that most Jewish weddings are on Sunday, so as not to interfere with the Sabbath, but I wanted to have it on Saturday to help my parents and others who were traveling get back to work on time for Monday, so we compromised on Saturday night after sundown.

Jeff had bartered with his friend Johnny Epstein to do the landscaping for our wedding in the backyard of Jeff's clinic (where we lived upstairs) in exchange for doing surgery on Johnny's dog. The morning of our wedding dawned and Johnny still hadn't shown up. If that happened now I would be a complete anxious mess, but at the time I was floating in a cloud of love and it didn't bother me in the least! Johnny came over about noon, while I was at the bridal shower, planted gorgeous day lilies and peonies and tulips and daffodils, and the backyard was a veritable garden of fresh blooms for our wedding that night.

So, Jeff and I got married, in the back yard of his veterinary clinic, under a chuppah and an oak tree, with Johnny Epstein's flowers around the base of the tree, twenty-five guests seated in folding chairs in the yard, and a few lonely dogs barking downstairs in the kennel.

My dear friend Cheryl stood up for me, and Jeff's friend Bob, from veterinary school, stood up for him. Betsy, another of my dear friends, took photographs. Our matchmaker Ron's wife Kat had lent me her exquisite tea length lace wedding dress, and I wore a small Southern hat with a curled brim, while Jeff wore an ivory jacket and khakis. Jeff's older niece, Rachel, was our flower girl. His younger niece, Michele, who was about two, can be adorably heard on the video, after her mother reminded her that she'd promised to be good, saying, "I want to be bad!"

A minister and rabbi jointly performed the service. I found a prayer that was used in both Christianity and Judaism—which was

"May the Lord bless you and keep you, May He make His face to shine upon you, May He lift up his countenance upon you, May He be gracious unto you, and give you peace." Unfortunately, the minister forgot I had asked for that prayer and used another one, and I was disappointed. I've remembered that for all these years. After our vows, Jeff stepped on a lightbulb and everyone yelled "Mazel Tov!" We had a figurine with two amorous cats on the top of our wedding cake.

One of his cousins and her husband didn't come because they were Orthodox and our small buffet reception wasn't kosher. Jeff and I weren't bothered. Jeff's father said, "What, would they only be coming to eat?"

It was funny, because my father was the family driver and he took care of all the money matters, and I expected Jeff, as my husband, to also take over those things. Meanwhile, Jeff's mother was the driver and took care of money matters in his family, so he was waiting for *me* to take over those things. So there was a vacuum in our marriage at first. The stereotype of Jewish people being good with money has not proved true with Jeff. He told me early on that he was obsessed with medicine but money matters did not come naturally to him. So I have done our finances for over thirty-five years (which my side of the family has found hilarious), and I did a lot of the driving in the early years of our marriage.

I love Jeff's family, which has been so welcoming to me. I love the Jewish traditions of lighting candles and saying prayers on the Sabbath. I love the traditional family dinners. I love the onomatopoeic and expressive Yiddish words that pepper his family's conversation, like "shpilcus," "tuchus," and "tchotchke." I love his family legend about his grandfather coming from Russia as a boy hidden in the engine room of a cargo ship. His sister has become like the sister I never had. Unlike my Protestant family, where I'd been taught to be obedient and well-behaved and to fit in, the Jewish culture of Jeff's family seems to celebrate individualism, self-expression, uniqueness. They joke that the reason there are 613 commandments for Jewish life is just so people can break them. So, maybe that same spirit of rebellion that I'd admired in Howie way back in middle school is also in Jeff. I learned in Judaism there is a beautiful concept called "tikkun olam," which means "fixing a broken world," which is what some devout Jewish people feel called to do. I remember feeling very emotional when I learned of this beautiful concept.

Our marriage was at first blissful. I became pregnant with Caitlin after we'd been married about a year or so, and when she was born I agreed to have a Jewish naming ceremony for her. Jeff's parents chose her Jewish name. I believe it was after Jeff's father's mother, but unfortunately I've forgotten that now and neither Jeff nor Caitlin can remember, either. And when Kelsey was born, we had a naming ceremony for her as well. I believe she was named after Jeff's other grandmother, Rebekah. The fact that we didn't have a boy was fortuitous because the bris ceremony for a boy seemed to me to be a much bigger deal in the Jewish culture. Jeff can remember his Jewish name, Yisrael, because he was called by it in Hebrew school. But our daughters didn't go to Hebrew school, and we never had occasion to use them, and over the years they've faded from our memory. I regret that forgetfulness.

I remember on our first Hanukkah, I was confused about whether Hanukkah wrapping paper existed. Since I'd never celebrated Hanukkah before, I'd never noticed it. Once I looked, I found it everywhere in Maryland, where there's a pretty large Jewish population. In Mooresville, North Carolina, where we moved later, it was nowhere to be found.

When Jeff's uncle died that first year of our marriage, I did what, as a Christian, I'd been taught to do—I sent flowers. There was an awkward silence in his family when I mentioned it. They had forgotten to tell me that Jews do not believe in sending flowers – they are considered to be fleeting. I've learned since then to make a contribution to a charity instead for Jeff's side of the family.

As the months passed and Jeff and I grew to know each other better, we gradually learned more about each other's religious beliefs. One night after our first Thanksgiving, when we were talking before going to sleep, I told him about my emotional experience joining the church.

"I guess I'd like for our family always to celebrate Christmas in some way."

"I have no problem with that," he said. "I remember when I was a kid I asked my parents for Christmas gifts a few times because I felt left out of the holiday."

"Really? Did they give them to you?" I plumped my pillow and raised up on one elbow.

"Yeah, I think it was a truck or baseball cards or something like that."

"That really surprises me—especially with your dad."

"My dad probably would have done anything for me," Jeff admitted. "He's religious, but I'm not. I mean, I hate religion."

"You hate it?" That astonished me. My faith was a source of comfort to me. "What do you mean?"

"Every war ever fought has on some level been about religion."

"Well, maybe a lot of them, but a lot have been about money and power, too."

"Think about it. Religion does nothing but divide people. It doesn't unite them."

I pulled the covers up over my shoulders. This kind of discussion made me feel a little scared. I hadn't really ever had a discussion with someone who hated religion. How could I have married Jeff without knowing that he did? "You hate religion?"

"Yes. I think it's all a bunch of junk, one of the biggest scams perpetrated on mankind since the beginning of time. Just mind control for the masses. And guilt. People being made to feel guilty for every little thing they do. And we'd all be better off without it. I agree that people should treat each other with respect and follow the golden rule."

My heart was starting to beat harder than usual. "So . . . do you believe in God?

"No."

"You're an atheist . . . ?" I realized I was holding my breath.

"Yeah, I am."

I broke out in a cold sweat, completely shocked. I had accepted the fact that we didn't have the same religion, but I felt that God was God and we both believed, and that was what was important. I honestly hadn't known that I'd married an atheist. We were just so enamored of each other, and then our courtship and marriage were fairly quick, and we didn't really seriously discuss these things until after we were married.

"Why did you tell your parents we would raise our kids Jewish?"

He ran his hand over his forehead. "I don't know. To make them happy."

I pulled the covers tighter and turned away. I didn't really know what to do.

After that, we had heated discussions about whether God existed, or whether there was life after death. "Of course there isn't," Jeff insisted. "There is no God, how could there be life after death? This is it, this life we're having. Make the most of it."

I disagreed. I didn't think of God as a big, white-bearded guy in the sky, but I believed. I thought of God as a presence—possibly female—in every living cell on Earth. The incredible beauty and complexity of nature and the goodness in people tell me every day that God exists. God is a humming, a loving presence in the universe. And I do hope that we go to join that presence once we die, become part of that humming energy. And do we see the people we've lost—our parents, friends, loved ones? I am not sure about that, but I haven't ruled it out.

Jeff feels all of that is ridiculous.

At any rate, learning that religion was not important to Jeff, and that he was, in fact, an atheist, made me rethink my earlier agreement to raise the children Jewish. I wasn't willing to be taking our children to synagogue and Jewish day school if he wasn't even going to be there with us. That seemed hypocritical.

It's natural, when we have children, to want them to reflect our values and to have beliefs like ours. There are jokes about moms who want their daughters to be "mini-me's," and dads who want their sons to achieve things, both in sports and careers, that they aspired to. Plays and novels abound about this very topic. I admitted that was something I yearned for, also. Yet, I had married a man from another religion.

I began searching for an answer. I didn't feel comfortable raising the children Christian, since I had earlier promised to raise them Jewish. Then, as synchronicity would have it, we got together with Ron and Kat (our matchmakers) and their parents, Jeff's aunt and uncle. And in a very casual aside, Jeff's aunt said, "You know, Lisa, we have attended the Unitarian Church for many years and we love Star Island."

I thought, what is the Unitarian Church, and what is Star Island?

So I began to research. I found that there was a Unitarian Church near us, in Rockville. Star Island is an island off the coast of New Hampshire maintained by the Unitarian Church for retreats, and Jeff's cousins had been going there every summer for years. In the Unitarian Church, I was elated to find what seemed to be an appropriate compromise. Both Christian and Jewish holidays were honored there. The Unitarian belief in the essential worth of every human being was also part of my own belief system. Some Unitarians believe in God, others don't. The Unitarian Church does not declare that Jesus is the son of God, but it does espouse his teachings. I began to attend the Unitarian Church of Rockville and took both children with me. I had both children blessed and joined the Unitarian Church one Sunday. It was quite a devastating experience for me, because Jeff refused to attend. I begged him to come, and I literally fell apart crying, but he stood firm and would not come. I'm sure the children were confused to be standing at the front of the church with a weeping mother.

On that day, I must admit, I didn't know how I felt about our marriage. I'd been doing a lot of reading, and much of what I'd read said that children should be raised in one faith; according to some experts, trying to teach them two faiths results in confusion. That made sense to me at the time, though since I've thought that children can learn two languages so why can't they learn two faiths? I think the gist of the thought was that with faith, if you're taught that there's more than one way to believe, then perhaps you won't buy any of it. So, by myself, since Jeff refused to be involved, I had chosen the Unitarian Church. I attended, took the kids to Sunday school, and I even taught Sunday school there. I was involved in the community. But Jeff wasn't, and he didn't see any reason to attend the service where I joined the church with the children.

I told my mother about it, dissolved in tears, and she advised me wisely. "Don't hold it against him," she said. I tried not to, but I believe I still did for a long time. Yet I have remembered her advice all these years, and appreciate her so much for it.

Ironically, I met a woman at the Unitarian Church whose

husband enjoyed acoustic guitar, and composed songs. I invited them over for dinner with their children, and Jeff and John ended up playing guitar together all night. And then they started getting together every Sunday afternoon. Eventually the two of them played at the Unitarian Church, and at other coffee houses as well. So, while Jeff didn't come to the Unitarian Church through faith, he did get there through music.

Taking the children to the Unitarian Church led to the only conflict that we ever had with Jeff's parents. When it happened, Caitlin was about four and Kelsey was a toddler and I suppose Jeff's parents felt that we should have joined a synagogue by then or started Caitlin in a Jewish day school.

Jeff's parents came over for dinner one night and when they came in we could tell that his father was angry. His normally pleasant face was red and his eyes were narrowed with concentration—as if there was a message he was determined to give.

"You need more Judaism in this household," Ike told us. "You led us to believe that you would be giving your children a Jewish education."

Blood rushed to my cheeks. My hands began to tremble. I looked to Jeff, whose face registered the shock that I felt.

"We don't blame you, Lisa," Etta added. "We blame Jeff."

Our girls had been greeting their grandparents, and I was getting ready to suggest to them that they go down to the playroom for a little while, but they ran out of the room on their own when they sensed the high emotions.

That night was a difficult night, but Jeff stood up to his parents and told them his feelings about religion. Though he didn't admit to his parents that he was an atheist, he emphasized that religion was not important to him.

"I've been taking them to the Unitarian Church," I said. "Judaism and Christianity are both honored there."

They seemed unimpressed.

"I really don't want our girls to be brainwashed with religious education," Jeff said.

"Judaism isn't brainwashing!" His father sat down, wiping his forehead with his handkerchief, breathing hard, his feelings overwhelming him.

I have to admit, I left the room at this point and missed the rest of the argument. I wanted to check on the girls in the playroom, as well as dinner. My head was roaring with anxiety. The dinner I served that night must have been horrendously overcooked. Our conversation must have been so stilted and shot with tension I blocked it from my memory.

This must have been hard for Jeff's parents, because as a boy, he was a star in Hebrew School, so much so, he told me, that his parents at one time believed he might become a rabbi. They thought he would want to continue with his Hebrew training after his bar mitzvah, and go on to get confirmed like his older sister, but he surprised them and promptly quit.

After that night, his parents never brought it up again. We had a few awkward weeks, and then things seemed to go back to the way they were before. And about a year later, Jeff's father passed away. He was the more devout of Jeff's parents. He frustrated Jeff and the grandchildren because he doggedly followed every page of the Passover Seder service, whereas other men in the family would jovially skip large swaths of the service in order to get to the food quicker. He attended the minyan at synagogue every day. Though Jeff's mother maintained the cultural and family rituals, such as lighting candles and cooking brisket and other traditional holiday dishes, she seemed less devout to me, more practical, and she never said anything more to Jeff about a religious education for the girls while I was around. When Jeff's nieces, his sister's children, reached the age of thirteen, they had their bat mitzvahs, and we attended. But we didn't have them for our girls. I don't know how Jeff's mom felt about that.

Jeff's father died during surgery for an aneurysm. When a family sits shiva after a death, the rabbi comes over every evening and conducts a service and friends and family attend. Food and coffee are served. Devout Jews usually sit shiva for a week, while more reformed Jews may sit shiva for only three days.. Jeff and I thought we would be sitting shiva for three days, but in the end his mother decided to opt for the full week, probably in deference to her husband's devout beliefs. I was assigned to be in charge of keeping the coffee pot full, but after a few days, I found myself exhausted. As the non-Jewish daughter-in-law, and also an introvert, after the first three nights, I just couldn't bring myself to go anymore. I let Jeff go by himself. I look back on that and feel that I was weak, but at the time, with small children, I just couldn't keep it up. I know the tradition was established to try to make sure mourners weren't alone, and, like so many Jewish customs, was imminently practical. But I found it exhausting.

As a family, we celebrated the holidays of both religions. We attended synagogue on the High Holidays (Rosh Hashanah and Yom Kippur) with Jeff's parents. We celebrated Hanukkah and each year had a Passover Seder with his family. We drove to North Carolina for Christmas and Easter with mine. The girls loved both traditions and adored both sets of grandparents.

My parents were pretty silent about our religious choices. When we went to North Carolina for Christmas, my parents and I usually attended the Christmas Eve service at the Methodist Church and the children went with us. Jeff stayed home with my Uncle Reggie. But my parents made no efforts to teach them the tenets of Christianity, though I'm sure my dad was always focused on modeling Christian behavior. They presumed that was our department.

One thing I learned over the years from Jeff and his family is that Judaism is more than a religion. It's a culture. It's a way of thinking about not just religion, but about food, family, customs, traditions, language, philanthropy, even jokes. (I am reminded of the Seinfeld show about the guy who converted to Judaism for the jokes). Jeff insists that he's culturally Jewish but just not religious. It's an identity.

Of course, "Southern Protestant" is also a culture. Possibly because I grew up immersed in that culture, it seemed natural to me, like the water I was swimming in. It's certainly a distinct way of living. Easter bonnets and Christmas carols and following the teachings of the Bible. Philanthropy. Turning the other cheek, which was a favorite of my dad's. Being polite and proper. Going to the beach in the summer. Patriarchal families.

When Caitlin was ten and Kelsey was seven, we moved from Maryland to North Carolina for a number of reasons. We wanted to be close to my family. Jeff didn't want to manage a veterinary clinic anymore, he just wanted to practice medicine. There were also many more public options for college for the kids in North Carolina than in Maryland. He also wanted to escape the growing congestion of the Washington area.

When we arrived in Mooresville, North Carolina, the inability to find Hanukkah wrapping paper was the least of our problems. There was not a Unitarian Church nearby. There was one in the UNCC area, but it was forty minutes away, and so small and in need of members that they asked me to teach the second grade Sunday school class on the first time I visited. I must say, that somewhat alarmed me. The next closest Unitarian Church of any size was in south Charlotte, over an hour away. I was able to persuade the girls to go with me to that church by promising them they could listen to the Casey Kasem Top 40 Countdown on the way down. That worked for about a year, and then they both revolted and refused to go. I didn't push it. Spending two hours in the car to attend church was a lot, and we were too far away to really feel like part of the church community, anyway.

I started attending a Methodist Church that was about ten minutes from our house, and when my parents attended with me, on Christmas and Easter, the girls would often go with us too. But, for all intents and purposes, the girls' religious education ended when Caitlin was about twelve and Kelsey was about nine.

I did feel guilty about it. My faith has meant a great deal to me over the years and I wanted the girls to have a faith to help them through any hard times they might encounter. The girls, grown now, are generous and thoughtful. They're both deeply ethical and honest. They bring food to friends who are sick, they stay up all night helping friends find their lost dogs, they give to charity. They are good and kind and loving people. They live their lives as Jesus taught, treating others as they'd like to be treated. When books they read have Biblical references, though, they tend to miss them. They know the differences between the Jewish and Christian traditions better than most people, but maybe not as much about the individual belief systems.

I spent a lot of time reading and thinking about the concept of interfaith marriages, and how it might affect the children, so much so that one of my first middle-grade novel manuscripts was a story about a preteen girl who finds a cache of letters in her parents' closet that reveal that one set of grandparents, whom she never knew, were Jewish. In my story, there was a rift between the families and a lack of acceptance of the union, and the girl somehow manages to repair the rift and rediscover her grandparents. I spent about a year or two working on that manuscript, writing about the girl's quest for a family reunion. I realize now that manuscript was my way of working out these issues in my own mind, and also that it was a poor imitation of *Are You There God? It's Me, Margaret* by Judy Blume. I abandoned working on the story when I realized that neither Jeff nor my children seemed troubled in the least by the issue of religious differences. After all that work, I realized the only one troubled by trying to work it out was me.

And, as it turns out, Caitlin, our oldest, converted to Judaism when she was about thirty. It actually happened because she was having a hard time meeting guys and we jokingly suggested she go to a synagogue and visit the young singles' group there. Caitlin is unfiltered, outspoken, and individualistic (maybe a little like Aunt Blanche!) and we thought a Jewish guy might appreciate her more than the traditional Southern guys she was meeting. She did actually visit the synagogue, and did not meet anyone, but then really felt she fit in, and decided she wanted to convert. She took an adult class there, had a test and a "mikvah," which is a ritual bath, and she was taken into the synagogue one Sunday morning. Jeff and Kelsey and I and a few of her friends attended the sweet ceremony. It seemed like the right thing for her. She now enthusiastically identifies as Jewish, has been perfecting her Jewish cooking, like matzoh ball soup and brisket, and loves lighting the Sabbath candles each Friday night. Meanwhile, she met Josh, who is Christian. Their first micro-wedding, during Covid, which I officiated (with an online ordination) was a secular one. The second wedding featured a chuppah that she and Josh built themselves, as well as her grandfather's prayer shawl. Josh stepped on the glass and the reception guests danced the hora. Caitlin intends to raise her children Jewish. Josh isn't necessarily religious, but is a huge fan of Christmas. Their first Christmas he put up massive decorations, all in the blue and white Hanukkah colors. So the questioning and seeking and compromising continue.

Kelsey, who is now thirty-one, is an artist, and seems to still be a Unitarian at heart, especially on social issues, though she hasn't attended any church for many years. Her husband, Seph, a mathematician, is not religious. However, Seph did step on the glass for their wedding ceremony, also. Possibly their seeking and questioning will begin later.

Jeff's sister, whose husband converted to Judaism, raised both of her daughters Jewish. The older niece has now converted to Christianity, and is deeply involved in her evangelical church. Jeff's other niece observes Jewish holidays and strongly identifies as Jewish. So, interestingly, from two sets of sisters from the same family, come two who identify as Jewish, one who identifies as evangelical Christian, and one who identifies as Unitarian or possibly atheist. In past generations, parents raised their children in a certain faith and expected them to maintain it, and today that is no longer always the case.

Do Caitlin and Kelsey believe in God? Practicing religious rituals and believing are two different things. When I asked them, Caitlin said, "In my late twenties, I started studying Judaism to get more familiar with my paternal family's faith. The values and belief system made sense to me, so I decided to convert. Today, I cannot say I am devout in my practice. However, I am aligned in a cultural and values-based way. I choose to participate in my Jewish community by providing meals for congregants and celebrating the major holidays. I know everyone conceptualizes their version of God differently. My version is a feeling—the feeling I get when I'm on the front porch of my family's beach house and we're together listening to my dad play guitar to a playlist curated by my sister, when I'm making my grandmother's matzoh ball soup, dancing in the kitchen with my mom, or watching my husband play on the floor with my animals."

Kelsey said "I guess I believe in some kind of rhyme and reason. I believe in a 'oneness,' like we're all collectively working to be better.

People's response to Covid has made me not believe in that as much, though. Maybe just say that I believe in yoga."

Embarking on an interfaith marriage was probably quite a challenge when my Aunt Blanche Verra married Maurice Salomonsky in the 1940s, and it was still somewhat of an issue when Jeff and I married in 1985, but seems less of one today. Our society is much less religious now. We meet many more people who have no religious affiliation, and wedding officiants rather than ministers or rabbis are becoming more and more common.

I also feel that our connection to Christianity weakened when my parents died, and our connection to Judaism may weaken when Jeff's mother passes away. Is that a good thing, or bad? I am honestly not sure. On the one hand, it's so sad to see the loss of traditions. On the other hand, it's good when people find common ground and don't feel that differences divide them.

When Trump was elected, and there were some anti-Semitic groups making noise, and when there was that horrific shooting in the temple in Philadelphia, I became fearful. What might happen if anti-Semitism became more pronounced and out in the open in our country? In spite of my common sense telling me the Holocaust could never happen again, I was still worried and afraid. I thought about the poem by Martin Niemoller, "What Will You Say When

They Come for Me?" That poem shook me to my core when I first read it—about the person who didn't say anything when they came for the Communists, or the socialists, or the Jews—because he wasn't one of those. But then, when they came for him, no one spoke for him because there was no one left. Now, of course, my own family is Jewish, and if anything should happen, I must and will stand up, not only for my own family, but for any people experiencing unfair treatment.

I suppose I'll never know if certain people might have decided not to be friendly toward us, or if some may have avoided us because of Judaism, or if some have hostile feelings toward us. In fact, honestly, I don't even want to know.

Just recently, during the pandemic, I have had a yearning for more spirituality in my life, and have begun attending the virtual services of a fairly new Unitarian Universalist congregation in the Lake Norman area. As I sit at my computer and watch these services, I've found myself feeling emotional about the ritual lighting of the chalice, something that is done at the opening of every Unitarian service. Poetry is almost always included in the services, and folk music played on an acoustic guitar. Social justice and service are strong components of the Unitarian belief system. It feels a little like coming home. So, my beliefs, and my feelings of religious belonging, have evolved over my life, as my mother's did, and possibly this will be the new path I take.

Jeff and I don't talk much about religion or God. His views have, if anything, become even more anti-religion. When I was young, I assumed that I would share my religious beliefs with my husband, and that has not proved to be true. It has made our marriage more difficult in some ways, but certainly not as difficult as it is for some, who have had to give up family relationships, for example. To be honest, I have found, to my surprise, that it's possible to love someone completely, to share my life with him, and to still disagree about religion. Overall, we have a loving, strong marriage that has weathered cancer, mental health issues, and many other problems more mundane. We are soulmates.

I adore our family, and no longer feel guilty about not providing a better religious education for my children. I did the best I could, and am proud of what good people they have become. I believe that exposing them to both Christianity and Judaism as well as Unitarian beliefs gave them a broader and deeper view of humanity. Now, they're making their own belief choices.

In the end, Jeff and I have had a blessed life together and I thank God for that. Even if Jeff thinks God had nothing to do with it.

A Lifetime of Wardrobe Malfunctions

My husband deliberately dresses shlumpy. As a veterinarian, he wears scrubs to work. Dressing up means putting on good jeans, and no outfit is complete without pet hairs. To me, saving animal lives is way higher on the manliness scale than his fashion profile. But there are times in life when you must dress up. So, when we received an invitation to the bar mitzvah of the son of Jeff's best friend from college, I freaked. "You need a suit!"

"Can't I wear nice khakis?" he said.

"It has to be a suit." I dragged Jeff to a department store. He fidgeted and grumbled while the tailor measured and pinned.

I picked up the altered suit before driving to New Jersey for the event and said, as we were packing, "Maybe you should try it on?"

"We don't have time!" Jeff tossed the hanging bag in the back seat and slammed the door.

I didn't push it. That night, in our hotel room, minutes before the bar mitzvah party was to begin, Jeff put on the suit.

"Honey . . . ?" Jeff said uncertainly.

I turned to look. One leg of his pants was five inches shorter than the other. One hem broke over the arch of his foot and the other revealed four inches of his ankle.

"Are my actual legs different lengths?"

"How could they be this far off?"

"What can we do?" Jeff gave me a panicked look.

Nothing. There wasn't enough of a hem for me to pull out. Jeff gamely went with one short pant leg. He leaned to the left, like at Passover, to try to make them look even. When we sat, he crossed his feet at the ankles. He struck awkward poses and stood in the shadows. We did not dance.

Later, we told the story as an amusing anecdote.

Fast forward a few years, and that same boy was getting married. Once again, a need for formal attire.

"You need a tux," I told Jeff.

"Can't I just wear my suit?"

"No. The invitation says 'black tie.' That means tux."

"I'll rent one."

We were trying to save money for college for our girls and had a thousand other expenses. "Fine. But you need to buy some dress shoes. One of the cats peed on your old ones."

The weekend of the wedding, in a gorgeous hotel room overlooking the water, with the Boston skyline in the distance, Jeff put on his tuxedo.

"You look fantastic," I said. "They say clothes don't make the man, but wow!"

He had discovered that he could also rent dress shoes. A perfect solution, right? But when he put them on, and took a few steps, the left sole fell off, flapping as he walked, like a clown's at a kid's birthday party.

"Honey . . . !" He took a few galumphing steps around the room.

Not another wardrobe malfunction! And it was the Sobins, the same friends as before! I racked my brain. "Maybe the concierge has some glue. Hurry, the wedding starts in fifteen minutes!"

So Jeff threw on his running shoes, with the tux, and ran downstairs. As I buttoned myself into my dress, sweat trickled down my side.

I finished my hair and makeup. Waited ten excruciating minutes.

Finally, sweating and breathless, Jeff rushed back into the room. "No glue—but you'll never believe it, the concierge found these in the lost and found!" He held up a pair of worn black dress shoes.

"You're kidding. Do they fit?"

"Pretty darn close!"

The first time had been a funny story. This time, we didn't tell anyone.

A few years passed and the time came for the wedding of my dear friend's daughter. After two wardrobe malfunctions, my anxiety about our clothing had become rather intense.

Well in advance, we bought a suit and had it altered. Jeff tried on the pants to make sure they fit and weren't uneven. I bought him a new dress shirt and tie. We *bought* him dress shoes.

I bought a new dress, jewelry, and stockings that matched.

The night before the wedding, we drove to the Virginia home of mutual friends. After dinner Jeff came out of the guest room, crooking his finger at me with a concerned look.

Once inside, he opened his suit jacket hanging in the closet.

No pants.

We exchanged looks of horror. After trying on the pants, he must have hung them on another hanger instead of with the jacket. And I hadn't checked when I packed it.

"This just goes to show, I am not a guy who is meant to dress up," Jeff said. The next morning while I was at the bridesmaid's luncheon, our friend Danny took Jeff to a department store, the blue pin-striped jacket in tow. Danny had to take a phone call, though, and when he came back, found Jeff at the check-out counter with a pair of white khakis.

"No, no, no, they have to match the jacket!" Danny helped Jeff find blue pin-striped slacks and eventually all was well.

And the wedding was so lovely, and the band was so good, that we danced all night. We danced so much that halfway through the reception I went to the ladies' room because one of my shoes felt funny. Then, as pairs of Jimmy Choos and Manolo Blahniks paraded by my stall, the soles of *both* of my shoes completely disintegrated. In strange wax-like chunks, they fell away into my hand.

The *one* thing I hadn't bought new. Had Jeff's wardrobe malfunction virus been passed on to me?

I took a deep breath. Everyone was looking at the bride and groom, not at me. I took them off, and, on my way back out to the dance floor, slid them under the edge of a long white tablecloth, and danced barefoot into the wee hours of the night.

In the future maybe our daughters will get married. Should we hire a valet? Opt for barefoot and khakis on the beach?

Maybe we should just encourage them to elope.

Happy Points

My husband Jeff has been collecting happy points. They give them out at our grocery store. Considering all the thought that has gone into understanding what makes modern adults happy, it's comforting to know that to achieve happiness all you really have to do is go to your grocery store and spend a little money.

In this case, you receive one happy point for every ten dollars you spend.

The happy points come in the form of stickers that can be applied to a page, similar to green stamps. Jeff takes great joy in affixing these stickers. He volunteers to go to the store for random items, items we don't even need yet, and I watch him as he comes in brandishing tiny metallic squares. He licks them, and neatly adds them to the line of stickers we've accumulated. Then he pleasurably contemplates the prizes we will win once these happy points are redeemed. Once, after shopping, curious to see if I could capture a bit of his pleasure, I affixed the stickers myself. Jeff was visibly disappointed when he found out I had done it.

I have actually been in therapy for depression for the past year and it's frustrating to learn that achieving happiness, which for me has become so elusive, is, for my husband, a simple matter of buying a few dollars' worth of groceries and coming closer to the goal.

"What is the goal?" you may ask. Kitchenware. Small kitchen

appliances. When we perused the page showing the prizes, I pointed out to Jeff that there was nothing there we needed. He was undaunted. "We'll get things for the girls," he said. After several phone consultations with our grown daughters, we settled on the hand blender and the waffle maker.

When the promotion was over Jeff had proudly collected the maximum happy points. In a highly anticipated trip to the store, he took the sheet with our collected stickers to redeem for the prizes.

"Sorry," the clerk said when Jeff arrived. "We're out of the hand blenders and waffle makers. All we have are the 36-cup coffeemakers."

"When will you get more?" Jeff asked.

"Tomorrow morning, early," she replied. The next morning Jeff was at the store at the crack of dawn. Not early enough, however. All of the hand blenders and waffle makers were again gone. Or maybe they had never actually come in.

"When will the next delivery be?"

"Tuesday morning."

"Can I put my name on a waiting list?"

"No. First come, first served."

"So? Still feeling happy?" I asked Jeff after his second trip home empty-handed.

"They will not defeat me," said Jeff. "I will wear them down with my patience. I don't care if I have to go back ten times."

After his third trip, the store had finally begun a waiting list that was seven or eight pages long when they added my husband's name to the end. Jeff, just to be on the safe side, visited several other branches of the store and added his name to their lists, too.

"They said we weren't allowed to put our names on more than

one list," he confided when he got home, red-cheeked and a little winded with excitement. "But desperate times call for desperate measures."

After almost a month had gone by, I went to the store and checked with the manager. "Do you know when you'll be getting in the waffle maker and the hand blender?" I asked.

"They said it would be next week but I don't believe them," said the manager. "We'll never do a promotion with that company again."

"That's okay," said Jeff when I told him. "Having to wait longer for our prizes will just increase our pleasure when we finally get them. The key is that others will give up. They'll forget. We can't. Not when we've come this far."

Finally, finally, nearly two months after the promotion ended, we received the long-awaited call from the store manager informing us that our waffle maker and hand blender had arrived. My husband raced to the store, obtained our prizes, and delivered them to our daughters. Our daughters took them with that casual gratitude that children have, never knowing that the price paid for these little appliances was literally dozens of trips to the store. Like many of life's goals, the process of getting them eclipsed their value many times over.

"And are you happy?" I asked Jeff. "Have the happy points made you happy?" This essential question, the one I have been pondering about my existence for the past year, kept coming back to me.

"Very," he said. "It makes me happy to get free stuff." But Jeff knew what I meant. He put his arm around me and squeezed my shoulder. "You'll get it back," he said with confidence. "You just have to be patient." He experienced a depression several years ago after his father's death. He was hollow-eyed and listless for months and I, having never experienced anything like it, became impatient with him. He is not that way with me. His deep and loving empathy is sometimes all that gets me through.

He understands that today, for me, happiness is a word in which the very definition begins a soul-searching that involves therapy and medication and where the answer seems complex and unreachable.

Now, for him, happiness is as simple as affixing a shiny sticker to a sheet and turning it in for out-of-stock kitchen appliances that we don't really need. There is something magical about his ability to do that. And the fact that he's able to feel happy about happy points gives me hope that one day I will too.

Parasailing with My Daughter

We stood in line at the parasailing window.

"Singles or tandems?" the ticket taker said.

My daughter, Caitlin, who was leaving for college the next week, said, "I want to go by myself!"

I'd been hoping she'd go tandem with me. Since I've become a mother I've developed a fear of heights. On a recent family vacation I was unable to walk out onto the Golden Gate Bridge, and have tried to plaster myself against the wall on the observation platforms at most of North Carolina's lighthouses, especially the creaky ones.

"I really want to go alone," Caitlin said. I told her she could. After all, she was going to college. We'd packed up her stuff and her room already looked bare, with a jangling collection of empty hangers in the closet. There was a strikingly clean surface on the top of her dresser, which until a few days ago stayed cluttered with notes, pictures of friends and lead singers, earrings, hair ties, and free samples of perfume and makeup. In only a week she was going to be making her own decisions, setting her own boundaries. She wouldn't have me there to help her in college, so she might as well be on her own with this flying-through-the-clouds thing.

Which, of course, meant that I would have to go alone too.

We piled into the boat with another family and motored a ways out into the sound. The sun bounced off the water, the boat rocked, and the waves gently slapped its sides. Caitlin's face bloomed with high color from excitement and I was determined not to ruin it with my fear.

"Who wants to go first?" the boat captain asked.

"Me!" Caitlin said. "I'm a single."

"With the wind out there today you're too small to go single," said the captain. "We need you to go tandem. We need more weight. Is there anyone here who will go with you?"

I was silent. Of course I was willing to go with her, but she wanted to go alone.

Caitlin hesitated, her disappointment written on her face. Was it better for her to go with a stranger than with me?

"I'll go with my mom," Caitlin said.

"Great," said the captain.

Together we put on life vests and the crew strapped us into the tight, heavy harnesses. The captain hit the gas and we sailed up into the air so smoothly we almost didn't notice it had happened. The bay and the boat and the water and the waves and the houses shrank smaller and smaller and sparkled in the sun. The warm summer sky wrapped around us, blue and cloudless.

I thought parasailing would be loud, with roaring wind and a helpless sense of speeding breakneck through the air. I had thought my heart would be in my throat and that flying along up there at nine hundred feet would make me weak with fear.

But instead it was silent, peaceful, almost surreal. The water, which had been choppy with whitecaps, looked perfectly smooth from up here. I looked over at Caitlin and her expression was fearless and expectant as she surveyed the dazzling landscape before us.

"This is great, Mom," she said.

"It sure is, sweetie," I said, reaching for her hand. "Thanks for coming with me. I was kind of scared."

"I know you were," she said. "But see? It's fine. It's going to be fine."

We were so high, we could see the gentle curve of the horizon.

The Long View: A Photo Shoot

Our younger daughter Kelsey has begun taking photographs. She wants to establish herself as a niche photographer specializing in intimate weddings and elopements. Maybe I'm not objective, but I think her photographs are gorgeous. She has taken a few lessons, but is mostly self-taught, and her eye for capturing the emotion of a moment is exquisite.

In order to get some shots for her portfolio, she arranged a styled shoot in the mountains. The bride and groom were volunteers, actually already married for about six months. The hair and makeup artist and the florist offered their talents for free in exchange for access to the photographs Kelsey was going to take. She had borrowed a wedding dress and tuxedo from a wedding boutique. She had borrowed an arch from a landscaper.

A young man she knew was supposed to assist her with the shoot, helping to carry the arch and the photographic equipment, but he got an offer for a paying job about two days before and canceled on her. When she told Jeff and me about this, I was upset to think that she would have to drive to the mountains herself and make several trips up the trail in order to carry everything.

"We can help you," I said impulsively, forgetting, momentarily, my own terror about mountain driving. "I don't see how you can do that by yourself."

"I'll manage," she said. "Don't worry about it. Or I'll find someone."

"If you don't find anyone, call us," I said. "We'll help you."

The day before her shoot I still had not heard from her, so I texted, not really expecting her to need us. Hoping she wouldn't need me to drive in those mountains.

Did you find anyone to help you tomorrow?

She texted back, *Are you and Dad still up for it?*

Of course! I texted back. She told me to bring sturdy walking shoes and a jacket. The jacket seemed somewhat unbelievable since it was in the 90s at our house, but I didn't argue.

Of course there was now still the matter of telling Jeff about this, since I had impulsively offered our help without checking with him.

"How far up in the mountains is it? How long a drive?" he asked.

"She says about two and a half hours," I said. "Some place called Black Balsam Knob."

"Why can't she just take pictures in someone's backyard? Why do we have to drive all the way to the mountains? What have you gotten us into?" Jeff complained.

"She has no one else to help her. The guy who was supposed to help her canceled."

Jeff continued to express skepticism about the whole enterprise, and my terror of the mountains was lurking in the background of everything, but we ended up agreeing to be at her house the next afternoon at two o'clock to load the arch in the back of our Honda. Her goal was a sunset shoot. Sunset that night was at 8:34.

"Hi, sweetie!" I said, when we arrived, giving our daughter a heartfelt hug. She was dressed in cut-offs and a tank top with a flannel shirt tied around her waist. Her long, wavy hair with silvery highlights was wound into a functional bun on top of her head. She seemed relaxed considering all that we were undertaking that day. Certainly compared to me.

My husband hugged her and gave her an energetic pat on the back. "Now, where's this arch?"

She pointed out a seven-foot metal arch that broke down into four pieces—two sets of legs and two sides of the arched top—and together she and Jeff loaded it into the car. It just fit if we put one back seat down. Then we loaded her camera bag, accessories bag, food, water bottles, a blanket, and a bottle of champagne for the bride and groom, and we set off.

As we headed out, with Kelsey driving, Jeff was careful not to reveal his true feelings about the length of the drive to Kelsey. "So, how did you choose this place?" he asked casually.

"Oh, it's a spot that's a short, easy hike from the road, and the views are spectacular. We're going to set up the arch at the top of the trail."

"So, we're going to carry this arch up a mountain?"

"Yeah. It's an easy hike."

I didn't turn around to look at Jeff, sitting in the back seat, because I didn't want to see his face.

It is always a joy to spend time with our daughter and so the time in the car passed quickly as we headed out of Charlotte on Highway 74 toward Asheville. The terrain became hillier and I got a little nervous when we got on I-40 and climbed that mountain just outside of Asheville. We passed Asheville and then Kelsey turned off onto a small twisty road that wound its way up toward the Blue Ridge Parkway. As we drove the vistas became more sweeping, the drops beside the road more precipitous, with purple-hued clouds hugging the tops of the mountains.

"What will you do if it rains?" I asked Kelsey, gripping the hand rest.

"It depends on what kind of rain it is," Kelsey said.

"The wet kind," said Jeff.

"If it's a light rain we'll keep shooting. The rain actually softens the photographs and you can get some really good ones in a light drizzle."

We got onto the Blue Ridge Parkway and wound our way up and up the mountainsides. I was not afraid of heights until my children were born and ever since then I have been petrified. I was sitting in the passenger seat looking down over sheer drops with my heart in my throat. I had not considered that what I had volunteered us to do today could have me frozen with fear for hours on end.

It was closer to a three-hour drive by the time we arrived at Black Balsam Knob. There was no real parking lot but cars of hikers lined the highway near the entrance.

Jeff and Kelsey shouldered the arch and, on shaky legs, I carried the various camera and food bags. The pine-needled path at first sloped gently through a copse of black balsam trees, which is where the location earned its name. Then we emerged from the trees and a rocky path headed almost straight up to a bald knob above the tree line. We hiked a short distance up this steep path to a small plateau which Kelsey examined briefly.

"Let's stop here," I suggested, out of breath and feeling vertigo.

"I think it's prettier up on the next level," she said, heading back up the trail. The rocks were jagged and steep and Jeff and I struggled a bit climbing that last stretch.

Finally she found the perfect location she was looking for—a plateau of rocks outcropping over a magnificent vista of mountains wreathed in purplish gray clouds with shafts of sunlight peeking through. The view was truly breathtaking.

We assembled the arch so that the sun could set just behind the happy couple. Then, Kelsey and Jeff headed back down the mountain to get another load of supplies and meet the florist while I watched over the camera equipment and the arch.

While they were gone, the clouds surrounding the other mountains began to drift over toward our mountain. At first, scraggly scraps of fog drifted by, giving me a chill as they passed over my skin. I put my jacket on. Then the scraps of fog became larger and more substantial.

As I waited, quite a few hikers passed by. A woman alone wearing a turban. A mother and her son, who looked about eight or nine, carrying large backpacks and a tent. A father and grown daughter who were built almost exactly alike. Two couples, including a woman who was pregnant, stopped and posed for a picture inside the arch, with the father's hand lovingly on the mother's lovely pear-shaped stomach.

Everyone was friendly. Everyone asked if I had brought the arch up and what it was for. One woman said there had been two weddings on Black Balsam Knob just the previous day.

Finally Jeff and Kelsey reappeared with the florist, carrying the boxes of flowers to decorate the arch.

"I am in my seventies!" the florist exclaimed as she huffed and puffed up the hill. "This is no easy hike. I almost did not make it!"

Jeff and her husband had literally pulled her the last few feet up the path.

"Just let me rest a few minutes before I decorate the arch. I need to catch my breath."

The florist had made gorgeous arrangements in varying shades of purple to clip onto the arch. She put arrangements asymmetrically on each side and then wound ivy up the legs and around the top. The arch looked stunning when she was finished, and Kelsey took numerous photographs.

As the florist and her husband prepared to leave, they lent us clippers for when we would need to disassemble the arch later in the day.

"That is so kind and thoughtful, thank you so much," Jeff said.

The florist and her husband began to pick their way back down the path, holding hands.

"I've got to go down and meet the bride and groom," Kelsey said. "We have to take a few pictures down below on the path and then we'll be up here in about an hour."

She headed down the path.

Jeff had brought some spectator chairs that we used to take to the girls' soccer games. He set the two of them up and sat in one.

"This could be the most ridiculous thing I've ever done," he said as soon as Kelsey left. "We could be safely in somebody's backyard instead of on the side of this mountain."

I noticed he hadn't breathed a word of this to Kelsey. He revealed his true feelings when only I was around, which I thought kind of him. I was feeling doubtful myself, as the cloaked wisps of clouds floating by us seemed to be thickening and the temperature had dropped to the point where I was shivering even in my jacket.

We waited for Kelsey's return. And waited.

More people went by, mostly down the mountain now. One guy in a bandana stopped and looked at us sitting there waiting in our skeptical disconsolate way, and said, "Live in the moment. How often do you get to sit on a mountain beside a beautiful floral arch and watch the sun set?"

"How often, indeed," Jeff said.

A guy came by asking directions, showing us his map. He told us he was from Vietnam. We assured him we had no idea where we were. We told him we thought it was going to rain.

"In my culture rain is good luck," he said. "It is a good omen."

"I think we are going to have very good luck then," Jeff said.

We waited. The clouds had completely surrounded us now. We were socked in pea soup and we could barely see the floral arch, much less the gorgeous vistas beyond it. We could barely see each other or our hands in front of our faces.

Still, we waited.

Then the rain started. A little drizzle at first. Little patters of dark spots on the rocks. The temperature ratcheting cooler still so that my teeth were chattering.

Still, no Kelsey. No bride and groom. We tried to call and text Kelsey but the phone service was poor and we kept getting "Not delivered" messages.

Then the deluge came. The skies opened up and the rain poured down practically sideways in the winds. Lightning flashed and thunder boomed. No one was going to see a sunset tonight on this mountain.

We finally got Kelsey on the phone. She was still down below taking pictures of the bride and groom in the black balsam grove, where it was barely raining at all.

"We're going to break down the arch and come down," I said. "There is no way you're going to get any pictures now."

Soaked to the skin, Jeff and I began tearing the flowers off the arch. It broke my heart to destroy the florist's beautiful work, but there was no way we could get the arch down the mountain without breaking it down. We ripped away the gorgeous blossoms and threw them onto the grass. Maybe someone tomorrow would find and keep them. Then, as lightning streaked through the sky, we broke down that metal arch.

As we were starting down, loaded down with the arch and bags, Kelsey arrived, and she grabbed my arm to help me climb down the mountain. The rain was coming down so hard there were rivulets of water in the path we'd climbed up so we were wading in ankle-deep water all the way down. The rain on my glasses completely obscured my vision. I couldn't see my feet. Kelsey was practically dragging me down the mountain, her hand firmly clasping my elbow.

"Keep going, Mom. Keep going."

I was breathless, on the verge of stumbling, nearly blind, and soaking wet. I kept turning around to Jeff and saying, "Are you all right?" He was right behind us, carrying the top of the arch. It was like carrying a lightning rod in a thunderstorm.

I thought we'd never get back to the black balsam grove.

Finally, completely breathless, we arrived on level ground, and in the sheets of rain, loaded the arch into the car. Our windbreakers were soaked and Kelsey's flannel shirt, when she handed it to me, was so loaded with water it felt like it weighed ten pounds.

"Where are the bride and groom?" I asked as I collapsed, soaked to the skin, in the back seat of the car.

"They had to get the dress out of the rain. We might have to buy it," Kelsey said.

"Oh Lord."

Kelsey insisted on driving down the mountain. Because of the rain the windows fogged up and we struggled with the ventilation so that we could see as we descended the hairpin curves. Inch by inch we crawled down the mountain in the downpour.

An hour later we were back on 74 on the way to Charlotte and Jeff was driving and Kelsey was checking her camera to make sure it hadn't been damaged in the rain. It seemed that her case had protected it. Then she started flipping through the pictures she had captured. While she didn't have any of the couple in front of the floral arch, she did have many of the arch itself. And she had beautiful shots of the wedding couple in the black balsam grove.

"I can salvage this," she said. I had respect for her as a true professional when I saw her upbeat and positive outlook on what could have been such a fiasco.

Jeff and I arrived home about midnight, after dropping Kelsey off with the arch. We got out of our wet clothes. He poured himself a beer, and I poured myself a glass of wine.

"Whew, what an experience," we said. We sank into our kitchen chairs, relieved to be home safe and sound.

"I was terrified coming down that mountain in that deluge," I told him. "I thought we were going to fall and break a leg or a hip."

"Me too. Kelsey said that was an easy hike. That was not an easy hike."

"Maybe we're too old for this."

We laughed as the tenseness and fear finally dissipated and we were able to relax and laugh a little.

"My comment about the backyard stands," Jeff said.

I wondered how much we really helped Kelsey. Having us along, with all our doubts and fears, could have been a burden to her. I wonder how often the doubts of parents stand in the way of a son or daughter's success. I am so proud of who she has become, and so relieved that I haven't passed my fears on to her.

Over the following week, Kelsey posted all kinds of shots and funny stories about the "chaotic" shoot on social media, garnering hundreds of likes. And at the end of the week Kelsey texted us that Asheville Wedding Guide had written her and asked if they could feature one of her mountain photo shoots in their blog. We were thrilled for her.

I told her I would be happy to help her again any time on a non-mountain shoot. She said she'd keep that in mind.

II

In Sickness and in Health

In Sickness and in Health

Mom and I are talking on the phone one morning when she suddenly says, "I have to hang up. Every time I turn my back your father climbs on the roof."

I picture her small, determined figure as she heads out behind their lake house on this windy winter day. The lake is choppy and gunmetal gray.

"Jack!" she'll shout. "You're seventy-eight years old! You're too old to be up there!"

"I know how old I am." Dad shovels wet leaves from the gutter with his gloved hands.

"I'm hiring someone to do that. I'm going inside to call right now," Mom says.

"Don't you do that!" Dad stands upright, bracing himself against the steep pitch of the roof. He wipes a renegade shock of white hair from his forehead.

Mom glances up in his direction with her hands on her hips. "It's ridiculous for an old man like you to be doing that." She purses her lips and marches across the yard.

"I am not old! Just last week my doctor told me because of my swimming I have the pulse of a much younger man!"

"I'm going inside to make that phone call right now," Mom threatens.

"If you do that, I'll divorce you!" Dad shouts.

Mom hesitates, then continues across the yard. They have been married nearly fifty-two years. Once I saw a photo of them on their honeymoon in Quebec. Mom looked so lovely, idealistic, and girlish. Dad looked cold and wet. He'd just dived into some forty-degree Canadian lake while showing off for Mom. When I was a teenager Mom still sat in Dad's lap now and then, and he warmed her car every single morning before she went to work.

Two springs before, my brother and I sat with Dad in the waiting room to hear the results of Mom's cancer surgery. When her surgeon said he'd gotten clean edges, Dad covered his face with his hands and wept. For hours afterward his cheeks were shiny with tears. He slept night after night hunched in a chair beside Mom's bed as she recovered. When she refused chemo, he cried every day for a month.

While visiting last summer, I watched Dad place a vitamin, a calcium pill, and a beta carotene tablet beside Mom's juice glass in the morning.

"They're too big," she said. "They get stuck in my throat. I've had a wonderful life. If it's time for me to die, I'm ready."

Dad looked at her as if to say, "Please don't leave me." Then he cut the pills in half.

Later in the morning, Mom calls me back. "He told me he would divorce me if I hired anyone," she says. "But he's gotten down now, anyway. He's been working on that tree in the backyard for almost an hour."

Last year when an ice storm hit, a huge tree fell in their backyard. Instead of hiring someone to remove it, Dad has cut a foot or two off it every weekend. Now he's down to the thickest part of the trunk and the going is slower, but soon he will be finished.

"He's gone down to the dock now," Mom tells me. "He's going swimming."

"It's forty-one degrees," I say.

"I know," says Mom.

As it turned out, Mom's cancer never returned, and Dad came down with pancreatic cancer, and died four years before she did. But the way they cared for each other has always been the perfect model of marriage for me.

More Time

I watch her all morning, going from my office down to the bedroom where she sleeps on the top of the loveseat by the window. She is emaciated, her white fur matted and yellowed. I can barely see the rise of her side as she breathes, very slowly, in and out. When I stroke her, she meows faintly, and raises her head. Her amber eyes are sunken and unfocused.

"She's in kidney failure," Jeff, my veterinarian husband, told me yesterday. "Her blood values are terrible. She's hanging on by a thread." He said when he left this morning that he would bring back the injection for her from his clinic. I agreed with Jeff that it was time.

I check on her before walking the dogs at lunchtime. She is still in the same spot and her breathing is so shallow I can barely see the movement. When I come back through the yard with the dogs the boys from down the cul-de-sac walk across our yard, talking animatedly about something. I say "hi" to them and am incensed when they don't even look my way or acknowledge my greeting. "Hello!" I say loudly. They keep walking. I want to yell at them, make them take notice. I immediately feel ashamed by my behavior.

In the afternoon I plan to go shopping for Father's Day. I check on Pearl before leaving, making sure I can still see her side moving up and down as she sleeps. She is clinging to life, barely breathing. I leave, hoping she might die while I am gone.

I can't find anything I like for Father's Day. My dad, eighty-eight, has been going downhill. He was a physics professor at Wake Forest for forty years, beloved by his students and all who knew him. He has not had many physical health problems, but his short-term memory is going. "What time are they coming?" he will ask, five or six times in an hour. "Where are you in school?" he will ask my daughter, though he has visited the campus and has given us generous gifts that have helped pay her tuition. Last April I did his taxes because he can't figure them out for himself any more. I know I should merely be overjoyed that I still have him, and I am. Of course I am. There is a picture of him at Kelsey's college graduation party, looking like a lost school boy, which breaks my heart.

My mother has macular degeneration, so she can't see whether the stains have come out of clothes. They both have PhDs and they look like homeless people.

I want to buy my dad some clothes to wear around the house that will replace the stained and torn ones he is wearing. I go to three or four places, but can't find anything that seems loose and comfortable yet stylish. Nothing seems right. I am so upset that I don't know his waist size. In the past I've only bought him shirts and sweaters. How could I not know my father's waist size? I stand in the store, close to tears, feeling helpless and furious and sad at the same time.

I finally find a pair of sweat pants, some shorts, and a golf shirt (he still plays golf and shoots below his age!) and bring them home, though I know that I would probably take some things back the next day because I'm not happy with them. I just can't find anything that I am happy with.

I buy my mother some clothes, too, though I'm pretty sure she won't like them. I get my dad a Father's Day card, standing in the aisle of Walgreen's crying at every card I open.

As I'm driving home we have a terrible storm, the sky turning black and thunderous and bolts of brilliant lightning streaking down to the ground. Rain has started to spatter by the time I pull in the driveway.

I leave the bags on the kitchen table and go in to check on Pearl. The loveseat is empty. She is gone. Jeff said that sometimes they will hide when they are looking for a place to die.

My heart starting to skitter a bit, I look under the bed. She is crouching there, her emaciated body tense in the shadows.

"Hi, Pearl," I say. "Are you hungry?"

She meows.

I race in the kitchen and open some special expensive canned food I have been giving her for the past week and spoon it onto a plate. Back in the bedroom, I offer it to her. She turns her nose away. She comes out from under the bed skirt, her hind legs as thin as knives, swaying with weakness as she walks. I take her a bowl of water and she lets her nose bounce off the surface and laps a few times. I think her head might sink right down into the water.

Taking the dishes back into the kitchen, I hear Jeff's car in the garage. When I see his face my eyes start to throb. He has some syringes and a little plastic pet burial carrier. Without saying anything, I go to him and wrap my arms around him. He takes me in his arms and hugs me tightly.

"She got up on her own and went under the bed," I say. "She also went in and drank some water. So maybe it's not time. Maybe it's not today."

Jeff looks at me for a long moment, and softness plays over his face. "It would just be delaying the inevitable."

My throat starts to ache. "Okay, just let me take my walk," I say, and head down the street for the two-mile walk I normally take in the late afternoons. Though it's raining, I take an umbrella and trudge through the puddles. I take some deep breaths, and the knots in my brain seem to loosen a bit. When I get back, Jeff meets me in the driveway with the dogs.

"Our power has gone out because of the storm," he says.

So then, in the darkening house, we lay the towels on the bed, and I hold her. She is weakly struggling, and meows a little. We both kiss her and tell her we love her. We run our fingertips over her bony head. Then, Jeff tells me to hold her rear leg down so he can find the vein. He inserts the needle and a little blood goes down the thin catheter. Then he injects the syringe into the catheter and I see the blood retract.

And within three seconds, her head falls to the side and what was moving and alive becomes immediately still.

I put my face in my hands and scrub it with them and feel the hot tears leaking between my fingers and I can hear the horrible sounds that I am making, just so very awful and I am wrenched inside out. The anguish engulfs me. I feel as though all of my insides are pouring out.

As I struggle to catch my breath between sobs, I barely notice Jeff, with tears on his cheeks, slipping her into her little burial bag with gentle, careful hands. He hugs me again.

He has already dug the hole. We carry the little bag with her tiny frail body out to the yard where our other pets are buried. He lays her gently in the hole. He shovels the reddish earth on top of her. I place some gardenias I've snipped from the bush in the backyard on top of the fresh mound. Though the blossoms looked pearly and gleaming with life only minutes ago, the petals look brown and limp already.

I normally love the aroma from gardenias, but today I catch a whiff as I'm arranging them on the raw earth and it makes my stomach turn.

It's still light and the power is still out. We try to figure out what to do about dinner. I can't think. I show Jeff the clothes I bought my dad and he agrees that they might be too big, as my father has lost weight recently, and maybe I should exchange them for a smaller size tomorrow. He agrees that no matter what I have bought my mom, she probably won't like it.

We toast Pearl and cry, remembering her. She was sixteen. She was the world's most adorable ball of white fluff when we got her, but when she grew up she was not a sweet cat. She used to lie in wait for the other two cats to come in through the kitty door so she could swat them in the head. If I tried to brush her anywhere other than her head, she lashed out and sank her teeth right into my hand. If either of our other cats tried to sit on my lap when I came to bed she literally bit them in the ass, chased them away, and made sure that spot was hers. The other two, both bigger than she was, stepped aside when she headed for the food dish. They always let her eat first. Miss Pearl, the Queen Bitch, we called her.

As the sun sinks lower and the light on our porch turns copper, Jeff and I laugh about Pearl, admiring her fierceness, and then our talk meanders on to other pets that have passed away.

We decide to grill some steaks and put the vegetables in foil on the grill, too, so Jeff builds a fire while I light some candles. We decide we can eat on the porch, since it's so dark inside without the power, and we do.

I can't really taste the steaks. The corn wrapped in foil with butter and salt would normally taste pretty good but not tonight.

"How do people act, when you put their pets to sleep?" I ask Jeff. I probably have asked him this every time we have to put a pet to sleep.

"Some people just get runny noses and puffy eyes. Others get hysterical," he says. "I try to schedule it in the late afternoon so they won't have to see anyone while they're leaving."

"How can you do that, doesn't it wreck your whole day?"

"No, it's emotional, but I'm relieving suffering. It's the right thing to do. Prolonging things is just selfish on our part."

"It is?"

I'm not sure how I feel. Is it selfish, for me to want more time?

The boys who crossed our yard earlier today are in kayaks in the lake behind us, laughing. The plastic boats crashing into each other make a moaning sound.

The lightning bugs have come out and they float around our heads like tiny lanterns.

A bird sings.

As the sun sets, Jeff brings out his acoustic guitar and plays a sad melody on the porch, the pure bell-like notes swimming over to me in the dusk.

Then, the power comes back on.

Read 'Em and Weep

I buckle my mother and father into the car. They both have crumbs on their shirts, and I try to wipe them off a bit without them noticing. At Reynolda Road, I wait for my mother to instruct me to turn left, as she usually does. I wait for my father to make his usual observation about all the traffic. But both of them are silent. My underarms are wet. I'm not shaking, exactly, but my mouth is dry and I don't seem to be able to draw a full breath.

We are on our way to take memory tests that Dr. Mary Lyles, my parents' long-time devoted doctor, has ordered. If either or both of my parents have Alzheimer's, it will be diagnosed today. My parents have both been amazingly stoic and resigned. I have simply told them that Dr. Lyles says it needs to be done, and they have agreed. I've been surprised, because I thought they'd fight the idea.

At Dad's 90th birthday party, several of us made toasts. My brother and I didn't talk to each other beforehand about what we'd say, nor did we talk to Dad's golf buddies or physics colleagues. But every one of us ended up saying the same thing.

"Jack never lets anyone else win."

Dad was a fierce, diehard competitor. Many a family evening was spent playing United Nations, Monopoly, or Mille Borne, where he inevitably accumulated the most flags, the most hotels, or the most miles. The only other person in the family who could give Dad a run for his money was my brother. I usually came in a feeble third. Mom usually came in dead last, and after a few games she'd stand up and put her hands on her hips.

"I quit." She'd stomp into the kitchen or go sit on the couch and read.

We are escorted into a large patient room and met by Dr. Ariel Gupta, whose incredibly shiny long dark braid reminds me of a Disney heroine and makes me feel hopeful somehow. Dr. Gupta explains how the afternoon will unfold. For an hour, Dad will take a memory test while Mom and I will be interviewed about his recent behavior. After analysis of this feedback, the doctors will meet with the three of us and discuss Dad's diagnosis. Then the process will be repeated for Mom. The entire procedure will take about four hours.

When Dad leaves the room, I wish I'd done a better job getting the crumbs off his shirt. Dr. Gupta stays with Mom and me while Dr. Thompson, a tall earnest woman working hard to make Dad feel at ease, escorts him to another room.

Dr. Gupta then asks Mom and me about Dad's behavior. Does he get lost driving places?

Oh, yes, we say. We describe the times he's gotten lost trying to find the lake house, and the church, and other places he's been going for fifty years. The time Mom and Dad missed their anniversary dinner at the restaurant they had been going to for a dozen years because they suddenly couldn't find it.

Does Dad ask the same questions over and over again, such as what time is our appointment today? What time is Lisa coming?

Oh, yes, he does that constantly, Mom agrees. I remember that I did my father's taxes in the spring but he forgot that I had done them and asked over and over when I was going to get them done.

After an hour, Dad returns to the room, and the three of us wait while the doctors confer.

Dad beat us at Blackjack and Seven Card Stud, peppering his dealer conversation with pithy card shark expressions like "ante up," "down and dirty," "that's no help," and "read 'em and weep." He beat us at Hearts and Gin Rummy. He beat us at backgammon, saying, "Baby needs a new pair of shoes!" with every throw of the dice, and sending our bedraggled men back to home again and again. He beat us at croquet in our back yard, where he always claimed the black mallet and called himself "Big Black." He once sent one of my brother's croquet balls all the way through the back yard, down through the side yard, and it ended up across the street in a neighbor's yard. He beat us at Eight Ball and Rotation in our basement, where he hung his special black pool cue on a hallowed rack on the wall, and ran the table, sometimes never even letting us get a single turn.

Dad turned everything into a game. In the fall, he raked our abundant leaves into a maze formation, with paths from one side of the yard to the other, and all the neighborhood kids came over and played a made-up game of maze tag we called HogPog. On Easter, both with us and with the grandchildren, Dad didn't just hide the Easter eggs in the yard once. Once the kids found them, he'd hide them over and over again.

When Dr. Gupta returns to the room, she says to Dad, "Dr. Williams, have you had any times lately when you've gotten lost going to a familiar place? Have you gotten lost at all?"

Dad crosses his arms over his chest. "No, indeed."

"You haven't gotten lost at all? Going to your lake house? Or to church? Or to restaurants?"

"No, never," Dad says staunchly.

Mom and I exchange a look. Then I glance at Dr. Gupta.

"And, Dr. Williams, do you sometimes forget what your daily schedule is, and have to ask your wife more than once what your plans are for the day?"

"No."

I am beginning to feel humiliated for my father. And I wonder if that is why he is acting this way—to bluster through the humiliation.

"Well, your wife and your daughter say you do forget things, Dr. Williams."

I feel like a traitor.

"You did very poorly on the memory test. You were asked to repeat back five animals and you couldn't name a single one."

I want to protest to the doctors that my father, a leading physicist for forty years, has never cared much about animals so why should he remember them now? I want to cry for him. I don't know why I've brought him here, why it is so necessary for the doctors to make him admit to all of this.

When I was in elementary and middle school, Dad taught a summer Physics Institute to bring in extra money, and sent brochures to high school physics teachers all over the state. My mom, brother and I were his mailing assembly line. One of us would fold the brochure, another would stuff the envelope, and the third would wipe a sponge over the glue strip and seal it. We did this for hours until the entire stack of hundreds was finished. He never offered to pay my brother and me. We considered ourselves lucky to have such an important job and to be taking part in the game.

After we watched the movie *The Sting*, Dad turned trips to the hardware store into a game. My brother and I went to different aisles to get items Dad assigned us, and when we came back he would put his finger to the side of his nose like Paul Newman and Robert Redford sending secret signals. My brother and I wandered the aisles giggling uncontrollably; who could ever make a trip to the hardware store so much fun?

Dad loved to get a deal, and he must've gotten one on my first car. It was bright orange—a crossing guard orange, orange that could be seen from a satellite—with brown houndstooth seats and no radio; I had to carry a transistor radio in the passenger seat.

When my mother leaves to take the memory tests, and Dr. Gupta asks Dad and me to discuss times when Mom might have forgotten things, Dad again crosses his hands over his chest and firmly says, "Mitzi is solid. She doesn't forget anything. Her memory is perfect."

I look at my lap as my father is speaking. Does he not remember all the times Mom repeats stories? Does he not remember the time that Mom denied that their minister had remarried? The times she has gotten confused in the grocery store or a parking lot? Is it that Dad has forgotten instances when Mom's memory has failed? Or is he just refusing to throw his wife under the bus? Is it a form of loyalty he is showing, a form of loyalty he's shown over sixty years of marriage and that Jeff and I have often remarked upon? Dad is loyal to a fault. He will never be trapped into ever saying a single negative thing about his wife.

Dad excelled at many sports—handball, tennis, and of course, golf. He shot below his age in golf for most of his eighties, no small feat, and on a weekly basis took the quarters from his foursome. Even after his memory began failing him and he couldn't find his way to the golf course, his friend and golf partner Mr. Williard drove him there and he continued to win.

When the grandkids came down to my parents' lake house, Dad played with them in the water all day long. The most popular game, of his invention, a variation on Keepaway, was Bobbin Stick, where Dad stood waist deep in the water with an old stick and all five grandchildren tried for hours to get it away from him, splashing, diving, and lunging through the opaque and sometimes muddy lake water until their fingers turned into prunes. Of course, none of them ever won the stick. And then they'd lie down on the dock, completely worn out, and Mom brought them slices of watermelon and Cokes on a tray to assuage their defeated spirits.

People who visited my parents at the lake had better look out if Dad said, "Have you ever waterskied?" If the person unsuspectingly said no, that person suddenly was forced to spend the rest of their visit attempting to get up on skis.

Here Dad is, faced with all of these doctors, willing to go into the other room and subject himself to the humiliating questions about the lists of animals and colors. And while he is gone, Mom and I both snitch on him, tell the doctors about all of his failings. While he, when given the same opportunity, will not relinquish his solidarity with his wife.

My eyes sting, and I sniffle, swiping my nose.

All my life, my father has been a hero to me. And now, on this day he is being diagnosed with Alzheimer's, he has become more of a hero than ever before.

Dr. Gupta turns to me. "Do you agree with your father, Lisa, that your mother's memory still seems good?"

I hesitate, twirl a strand of my graying hair around a finger. How would my father feel if I snitched on my mother? I decide to make my answer nonverbal, so as not to alarm Dad. I meet Dr. Gupta's eyes and give my head an almost imperceptible shake of "no."

When in the 1990s the Physics Department at Wake Forest suffered from a dearth of students, Dad's competitive spirit rose to the rescue. He developed a "Physics for Non-Majors" class that ended up filling an auditorium. One of his signature lectures was the one on centripetal force, where he asked a student to fill a bucket with water and place it behind his podium. Then, as he lectured, he smoothly picked up a bucket, swung it around and around, then threw it out at the students. They all screamed and ducked. But of course he had substituted a bucket of shredded paper.

Dad's crowning competitive achievement was the new building for the Physics Department at Wake, which he won with a grant from the Olin Foundation. He worked on it for years, and applied more than once. He and the esteemed Wake Forest provost, Edwin Wilson, finally went to New York to secure this grant. I don't know how many other universities competed for the grant that year, but Dad and Dr. Wilson and Wake Forest won.

The doctors diagnose Dad with mild Alzheimer's. He has perhaps two years before a serious decline, they say. Their immediate concern is driving. Mom is legally blind, and Dad has only one good eye. He doesn't know where he is, and soon Mom won't, either. They should not be driving, the doctors tell us.

When I ask Dr. Gupta about my father denying having any memory problems, she assures me that my father's reaction is very common. "Many people deny having the memory issues. Usually, it's because they forget they've had the problems."

"So it's not denial . . . he's actually forgotten?"

"Yes."

I prefer to think of my father as being noble, and loyal. I decide I don't believe Dr. Gupta, realizing, at that same instant, that I myself, am experiencing a form of denial of my father's condition.

Mom is not diagnosed with memory loss, but the doctors do feel she has frontal lobe issues surrounding executive function. "Her decision-making abilities are very poor," they tell me. "Your parents are at serious risk, because your father, who has been making decisions for them all of these years, is no longer capable of making them."

I feel a tightness, a weight, a feeling of doom around my heart as I escort my parents back to the car. I agonize about how to discuss it with them.

The doctors tell me that my father, because he is so smart, has become good at confabulating, or pretending to remember things so people won't know he's forgotten. It is true, most of my father's friends and colleagues have no idea of the extent of his memory challenges.

Our daughter, Caitlin, when she was about four, stayed with her grandparents at the lake for a week. Dad had to go to the pharmacy to pick up a prescription, and while they were there he challenged Caitlin to a game of checkers, which happened to be set up on a small table in the pharmacy waiting area.

Caitlin called Jeff and me that night, crowing, exuberant. "I beat Da! I beat Da at checkers!"

Jeff and I looked at each other in disbelief. That wasn't possible.

"Put him on the phone," I told Caitlin.

Dad got on. "Ye—es?"

"Did Caitlin really beat you at checkers?"

"Yes, indeed."

"I don't believe it. Didn't you just teach her how to play checkers?"

"Yes, indeed."

"Sooo . . . she beat you, a veteran of eighty years of checker-playing, on her first attempt to play the game?"

"Yes, indeed."

I hung up and turned to Jeff, the bitter resentment of a long-time loser flaring, then seeping away as the sweetness of what had happened came over me. A miracle had occurred. Dad, after all these years, had finally let somebody else win.

Blinding Rain

Thunder roared, the early-afternoon Carolina sky turned black, and the rain gushed down in torrents.

"Goodness, this storm is awful," my elderly mother said from the passenger seat as I looked right, then left. When I saw no cars coming, I cautiously pulled out to make a right turn from the Harris Teeter parking lot onto Reynolda Road in Winston-Salem. Immediately I heard a "thump!" and saw something fall to the ground beside my left bumper. A young woman had walked out in front of my car from the right, while I paused, looking for traffic from the other direction, and I'd hit her.

"Oh my God!"

"Lisa, what's that?" Mom had macular degeneration and couldn't see out of one eye. Not to mention the blinding sheets of rain.

I slammed the car into park, jumped out, and helped the young Black woman to her feet. "Are you okay? I didn't even see you." Rain soaked us, poured into my eyes. "I am so sorry!"

The young woman quickly gathered from the wet pavement a brown bag, a liquor bottle broken into two or three large pieces, and a sandwich. Blood from her knee ran down her leg and mingled with the rain.

I grabbed the umbrella from my car door and held it over both of us. "I'm so very sorry. Let me call 911 in case you're hurt." As soon as I called, I gave my location and told the dispatcher that I had accidentally hit someone. The dispatcher told me to stay where I was and that an officer would be there shortly.

"Can I sit in your car, since it's raining so hard?" she asked.

"Sure." I opened the back door and she slid inside. I stood waiting for the police, listening to the rain pound onto my umbrella. She put the broken liquor bottle pieces on the floor of my car.

Should I take her to urgent care? I didn't see how I could do that with my elderly mother in the car.

"Can I use your cell phone to call my boyfriend to come get me?" she said. "Just one call." The girl was wet from head to toe, as she had no umbrella and no raincoat, and her hands shook as she tried to rewrap the sandwich. "I was taking my boyfriend his lunch."

My hands were shaking too. I couldn't believe I hadn't even seen her and that I had hit her! What a tremendous relief that she appeared to be all right, except for the scraped knee. But I didn't want to let her use my cell phone.

"When the police get here I'm sure they'll let you use their phone," I said. "They should be here any minute."

If she had been white, would I have let her use my phone? I don't think so. But I still wonder about my own reaction. Was it racist? Only a week before, I'd read an article about people deliberately walking in front of slow-moving cars in parking lots in order to get insurance pay-outs. Was that what this was? And again, if this person were white, would I have thought that?

The drenching rain stopped as suddenly as it began. The police arrived within about five minutes, and when they arrived, one of the officers asked the girl to get out of my car. As she climbed out, she gathered the sandwich but left the broken liquor bottle on my car floor.

"That's not mine," I told the officer. "It's hers." I wasn't going to have him suspect me of driving under the influence. It was enough that I had hit her.

"Why don't you get that bottle out of her car?" the officer instructed the young woman, so she gathered up the broken liquor bottle pieces, again, with shaking hands.

"So, tell me what happened," the officer said to me.

"Well, I'd just taken my mom to Harris Teeter to get some groceries and I was headed back to Salemtowne, where she lives."

The police officer leaned down to look at Mom through the car window and she hesitantly smiled at him.

I added that I had looked for traffic both ways, and when I didn't see any cars coming from the left, I pulled out to turn right.

"So you didn't see her at all?" the officer asked me.

"No, it was pouring. Also I guess I just wasn't expecting a pedestrian coming from the right." Was there even a crosswalk there?

"Did you see the car when you headed across?" the officer asked the young woman.

"No." She shook her head. She looked close to tears.

The officer filled out a form, tore off a copy, and handed it to me. "You're free to go."

"You'll let me know if she has to go to the hospital or anything? I feel so terrible, I really hope you're not hurt." I got back in the car with Mom and, practically hyperventilating, drove away. In my rear view mirror I saw the officer still talking with the young woman.

"What in the world just happened there?" Mom asked.

"I just—I don't know, I just hit her. I didn't see her at all. Thank goodness I was barely moving."

"You were such a quick thinker, calling 911 so quickly, and then not letting her use your cell phone. How did you know to do that? I don't think I would have."

"I had no idea what I was doing. I guess I could have taken her to the hospital or a doctor or something. I just feel terrible about the whole thing. Gosh, I hope she's okay."

"No, I think what you did was right. Just let the policeman handle it." Mom pursed her lips and stared straight ahead. Before integrated schools, Mom taught in a Black high school for many years and had great fondness for her students. She still had some old-fashioned attitudes about racial differences but she was more socially responsible than I have ever been. My parents, both educators, were eager for me to have the best education possible. I left my integrated high school, and went to a prestigious private university. I'd led a privileged life. And I was no stranger to drinking. I had been pulled over once in college, and have never driven after drinking since.

After I got Mom settled in her room in assisted living, and climbed back into my car for the drive home, I gained the courage to look at the form the policeman had given me. He had checked a box saying "no charges applicable."

I have gone over this incident in my mind so many times. Did I do the right thing? Should I have let her use my cell phone? What if the young woman had been white and I had been Black? Would the officer have let me go?

I have wondered so many times whether the young woman was indeed all right. I don't know if she had been drinking when she walked in front of my car, or if she was truly taking the sandwich and the bottle of liquor to her boyfriend. I don't know if she was simply trying to hide the bottle from the officer when she left it in my car. Even if she had deliberately walked in front of my car to get an insurance payout and planted the bottle, I still felt horrible that a person would feel they had to do something like that to survive. I just think back on her and remember a desperate person and feel regret. I wonder what happened to her.

Once I even went back to that same intersection to see if there was indeed a crosswalk. And there was.

I might have taken her to the doctor. I might have gotten to know her. I've read inspiring stories about people in situations like this who have ended up having lifelong relationships, both benefitting from what the other could bring to the table.

I wish I had seen her.

Resist

As I passed by the dining hall in the assisted living center where mom ate her meals, I smiled to myself, remembering a conversation with my twenty-eight-year-old daughter, Caitlin, after she ate dinner with her grandmother.

"Grandma sits at the mean girls' table. They talk smack about the ones who have dementia. Like *they* don't have it! You'd think that people would learn by age eighty-five that high school cattiness doesn't pay," Caitlin said.

"They probably did learn," I said with a rueful laugh, remembering Caitlin's misery in high school. "But they forgot."

I arrived at Mom's room and knocked gently as I pushed open the door.

"There you are," Mom said, looking up with a wan smile from her newspaper, her face only inches from her large magnifying glass. I still felt guilty that I'd moved her into this one room, with the same bed she and my father had slept in, one nightstand, one dresser, a couch, a rocker, and a TV. Yet there had been nothing else to be done.

"Are you ready, Mom? Let's go so we're not rushed for your doctor's appointment."

"But you're going to make your presentation after we get back, aren't you? The ladies at my table want to know all about the march."

"Uh . . . sure." I had not in fact prepared a presentation because I thought Mom would forget. Clearly that hadn't happened.

I'd never been a political person. I'd been a college student in the seventies, lived through Vietnam and Watergate, and never marched about anything. But when one of my writer friends mentioned going to the Women's March on Washington a few weeks ago, I had an overwhelming urge to go. So I went, even though my husband was fearful it could be dangerous. It was actually an exhilarating experience, possibly life-changing in jolting me out of my complacency, but I'd never dreamed that the women in assisted living would want to hear my account of it.

I glanced at the portrait of my father above Mom's bed. I'd painted the portrait myself at about age fifteen, at Dad's request. In it he wore a beautiful sky-blue shirt, and he looked stern and gray-haired. My grandmother had not liked the portrait. "My son never looked that stern a day in his life!" she'd exclaimed. My father claimed he loved it and somehow out of all the possessions we chose to bring to assisted living after Dad's death last year, this portrait survived and won a spot over Mom's bed. My father did indeed look strict in my amateurish portrait, but if I studied it, I could eventually see the ghost of a smile. I checked the portrait every time I visited, hoping to see the smile and read into it my father's approval for the way I was caring for my mother.

I aimed my mother's new walker in the right direction.

"No, no, I don't need to take that thing," Mom exclaimed. "I'll just take your arm. I pride myself on my independence."

"Mom, if you're holding onto my arm, you're not independent," I said. "You need this walker."

"No, no, I don't need it!"

"Yes, you do!" I could feel sweat under my arms and at my hairline, but after a tense discussion, my mother finally accepted the walker and we rolled down the hall. In the lounge beside the elevator, Mom waved to two women from her table in the dining hall. "Everyone, this is my daughter, Lisa!"

I had met Jane, a tall straight-backed woman with iron-gray hair, several times.

"So nice to meet you," Jane said, nodding at me.

I had also met Margaret, a rounder woman with excited eyes who was always smiling. "So nice to meet you!" Margaret enthused, jumping up to shake my hand.

"So nice to see you." I didn't add "again."

"Lisa's going to share her experiences at the march in Washington when we get back from the doctor's," Mom said proudly. "I hope you all will come! Now, Lisa, I want you to come down the hall to meet my other special friend." Mom pulled at my hand. "She said she's heard so much about you and is extremely eager to hear your presentation about the march."

"Do you mean Bitsy, Mom?" I had also met Bitsy. Once Bitsy had visited in Mom's room for over an hour, talking about the sons she adored.

"Yes, Bitsy! She'll be beside herself if she doesn't get to meet you."

I stopped my mother. "Why don't I meet her when we get together to talk about the march?"

"But you have to meet Bitsy!" my mother cried, with a look of consternation. "She is so eager to meet you!"

I drew a deep breath. "Okay." I accompanied my mother down the hall. Bitsy was not in her room, and Sara, the nurse, as she passed, told us that she had gone for her daily chemo treatment.

"She is excited about your presentation, though, Miss Lisa, and will definitely be back," Sara assured us.

I began to get nervous about this presentation. I wished my mother hadn't built it up so much.

Once the two of us were alone inside the elevator, Mom slumped against the wall with the most pitiful air of despair and resignation. "What am I going to do, Lisa?"

Was Mom feeling a sense of loss and confusion? What kinds of words of reassurance could I offer? While meeting the assisted living residents anew with each visit felt a bit comical, like in *Groundhog Day*, or *Fifty First Dates*, I also felt close to tears. It broke my heart to see Mom become more and more child-like. But I wasn't sure what my mother was referring to, so I just said, "What are you going to do about what, Mom?"

"All these people around here with their terrible memories! I try to have a social life but no one can remember each other's name much less any plans I might try to make. The conversation around the table is so boring. Everyone says the same things over and over. And even if you say something interesting no one can hear it!" Mom drew herself up, all five feet of herself, with a huff. "I'm just used to being around more scintillating conversation."

My eyes stung and I looked away, pretending to check the elevator button. I'd cried in the parking lot for a good twenty minutes after my first meal in the dining hall with Mom. At the same time, now I fought a small impulse to smile. I was thrilled to hear Mom use the word "scintillating." And leave it to Mom to think that memory loss was everyone else's problem but hers! "I know you feel frustrated, Mom." I tried to give my mother an answer that would satisfy her competitive nature. "But I think you're sitting at a good table in the dining hall. Even Caitlin remarked on it. The conversation hasn't been too bad when I've been there."

"Not like I'm used to." My mother had always set great stock in lively conversation. She had told me when she was younger that her greatest, deepest wish was to be an intellectual, and she'd read voraciously and made efforts to surround herself with accomplished and articulate people. She went back to school in middle age, earning her PhD. "But I must admit, your presentation this afternoon will be diverting and we're all looking forward to it. My special friend—"

"Bitsy—"

"Yes, Bitsy, is especially eager to hear it."

"Well, good, I'm flattered." I helped Mom into the car, buckled her seatbelt, and loaded the walker into the trunk. "Do you remember Dr. Patel?" I asked as I climbed in the driver's seat. Dr. Patel had to check Mom's eyes once a year, even though there was nothing he could do for her macular degeneration.

"I'm sorry to say that I don't," said Mom, as I headed out of the parking lot.

"You and Dad have been going to him for about five years. He had so much respect for Dad."

I glanced at my mother.

Mom avoided my eyes and looked out the window, silent.

I was looking forward to seeing Dr. Patel. He had been so caring toward my parents, particularly my father. There was comfort in seeing him again since Dad had died.

We got our number in the waiting room, where about twenty

other people waited quietly, reading and checking their phones. I managed the walker, and eased Mom into her chair.

"I'm reading another Jack Reacher book," Mom said, somewhat loudly, to me.

"Oh, good." I winced; Mom's reading tastes had been more literary in the past.

"There's a very interesting scene where he meets a female detective, and the very first thing she tells him is, there is not going to be any sex."

I glanced around the room. Every single person in the room had to have heard what Mom said. No one reacted at all, but people were doing a bad job of pretending they weren't listening. A white-haired man across from us folded his hands and looked at the ceiling. One woman smiled as she turned the page of a magazine.

"Oh," I said noncommittally. Maybe I could suggest that Mom and I could discuss this later?

"After that, I couldn't stop reading," Mom went on. "I knew if she said there wasn't going to be any sex then there would definitely be some. I can't believe it, I stayed up until four in the morning trying to get to the sex part."

Another woman next to us was pretending to look at her phone but she was smiling. The white-haired man's ears were perked up like a cat's.

"Four in the morning. Mom! You'll need a nap."

"Well, that was a pretty good trick, wasn't it? To say there wasn't going to be any sex and then get people reading, thinking there surely would be some. But sure enough, at the end of the book they just shook hands and walked away. Other writers can learn a lot from that Reacher writer, what's his name?"

"Lee Child."

"Yes, they could learn a lot from Lee Child. Has that ever happened to you, that you'd stay up all night reading to get to the sex scene?"

To my great good fortune, at that moment a technician called out, "Alice Williams?" The technician greeted Mom warmly, and led her into the exam room.

"Tell me which line you can see?" the technician prompted.

Mom could not even read the big *E*.

"Well, it's all right," the technician said jovially, patting Mom's hand. "Dr. Patel will be right in."

I knew Mom was going blind. But next year she would be ninety. The medical personnel who cared for the elderly had a special, more accepting approach to their patients, and I was trying to learn from them.

Photographs were taken of Mom's eyes, and then Dr. Patel came in, with his starched white coat and his kind face. "And where is Dr. Williams today? Why isn't he getting his eyes checked? It's very important for us to keep a vigilant look on that one eye."

Mom's mouth fell open but no sound came out. I could see my mother begin to collapse.

Quickly, I said, "Dad passed away a year ago. Last November."

Dr. Patel looked stricken. The color drained from his face. "Why was I not told? I am so sorry, I didn't know." The doctor slumped onto the stool and put his hands on his face, ever so briefly, then seemed to think better of it and sat up straight, his hands on his knees, with his eyes brimming. He turned away.

My heart nearly broke to see the shock on this young doctor's face. I'd thought that Dad's death would have been communicated through the hospital's online health care portal. "I'm so very sorry. I assumed other people in the hospital would have told you."

Dr. Patel shook his head back and forth a few times, overcome.

"You took such wonderful care of Dad, Dr. Patel," I said. "He had such faith in you."

Dr. Patel stared at the floor. I glanced at my mother, whose eyes looked ghostly. I felt the pressure building up in my own eyes, a burning in my throat and my nose beginning to run.

For a moment or so, Mom and I, and Dr. Patel, all cried together. It seemed that the tears lifted up into the air and gathered with each other into an invisible cloud, cleansing and easing the room. Then wafted away.

Dr. Patel cleared his throat and clapped his hands on his knees. "Well, let's see how your eyes are doing, Mrs. Williams. We just got your photographs back." He moved the scope over Mom's face. "Look straight ahead. Blink."

"I don't believe I can see a thing," Mom said.

There was silence in the room for a few minutes while Dr. Patel examined the photographs of Mom's retinas and made measurements. Finally, he said, "The macular degeneration is progressing, but I'm afraid there's nothing I can do. I wish I could, but I can't."

"We understand," I said.

My chest still ached as I guided my mother's walker through the parking lot to the car. On the way home, I said, "So, Mom, I know you said you didn't remember Dr. Patel, but when you saw him, you remembered him, right?"

We were at a light and I was able to look directly at Mom. Her eyes went wide.

"No, not really." Mom took a breath, looked down, and carefully adjusted her purse over her shoulder.

When we returned to assisted living, I walked my mother to the small library on the first floor of the main building to see if we could find any large-print books Mom could read with the magnifying glass I had gotten her.

"I think I've read every Jack Reacher book they have here," she said mournfully as I combed through the collection of large print paperbacks. "Do you know when he's coming out with a new one? I finished that whole book last night."

Without ever getting to the sex scene, I reflected with a small smile.

Mom had been in the university book club all her life. Somewhat of a snob about her reading material, she had voraciously read classics, and literary novels, and prodded me into discussions about them at the dinner table, especially after I majored in English in college and decided to teach literature and write. In recent years, I had begun ordering books for her on Kindle, and one day was shocked, after ordering *Madame Bovary* for my mother, to hear her complain.

"I don't like that book *Madame Bovary* that you gave me at all. Whoever wrote it goes on and on about nothing. That writer could learn a lot from Lee Child. He really knows how to keep the action moving."

I didn't admit it to Mom, but my feelings were hurt. Why was my mother going out of her way to tell me she didn't like the book? Furthermore, how could Mom's literary taste have changed so drastically? The same thing happened a month later, when some of Tolstoy's books were available for under a dollar and I sent *Anna Karenina* to my mother's Kindle.

"That book *Anna Karenina* that you gave me is so tedious! Can't you find any more of those Jack Reacher books?" my mother complained. "That Leo Tolstoy just goes on and on ad infinitum. Not only does he give every thought that goes through the main character's head, he gives every thought that goes through every other character's head, too. He could learn a lot from Lee Child."

"Well, maybe I shouldn't get you any more books, since you don't seem to like the ones I've been getting," I snapped.

"Oh, don't say that, darling!" my mother cried.

I immediately felt ashamed for losing my temper. Yet, the first thing I did was order a large-print edition of Edith Wharton's *The House of Mirth*, remembering an animated discussion about it we'd had once at the beach. That book had shaken me deeply; the tenuous plight of a single woman had been so harshly portrayed I had replayed scenes from it in my mind for weeks. I'd tried to express this to my mother on that beach walk. The next time I visited Mom, though, she gave it back, pronouncing it extremely tedious.

As I was helping Mom unlock the door to her room, I saw Bitsy hurrying down the hall. She greeted Mom fondly, then said, "Are you Lisa?"

I smiled and shook her hand. "Yes, hi, Bitsy, great to see you."

"I'm so delighted to finally meet you!" Bitsy said. Her flyaway silver hair seemed like a halo with a mind of its own. "I can't tell you how excited we are that you'll be sharing with us about going to the march in Washington. We all need to resist! It's essential!"

I shook my fist fiercely. "I agree!"

The lounge was one floor up, just outside the elevator doors. Once inside, Mom sat on the loveseat and let me and Bitsy arrange a few easy chairs in a semicircle to accommodate about ten people. Would that many come? I had imagined it would be only two or three.

"I read the *New York Times* every day," Bitsy told me. "And it's just appalling, we have to do something, we simply can't stand by and let our democracy be destroyed like this."

"I agree!" My heart swelled with fondness for Bitsy's enthusiasm.

To my surprise, women drifted into the lounge one by one, stowing their walkers like soldiers by the door. By the appointed hour of two, eight white-haired women in varying stages of alertness, including my mother's friends Margaret and Jane, sat in a semicircle around me. I sat in a rocking chair up front, feeling shaky from the initial burst of adrenalin that always occurred before I had to speak in front of people.

"Thank you, everyone, for coming today. I'm so pleased that you're interested in hearing about my experiences at the Women's March. I should tell you that as a young woman I didn't have any interest in protests, though I've always considered myself a feminist. For most of my life I've taken our democracy for granted, but this election has opened my eyes. Many of our freedoms are being challenged, and we must be vigilant to make sure our system of government survives."

"We want to hear about the pussy hats," said Margaret, with a big grin, her eyes sparkling.

"The what kind of hats?" said Jane, her eyes wide.

"Oh, I know what those are," said Bitsy. "They wrote about them in the *New York Times.*"

"What are they?" said Jane. "I've never heard of them."

I felt my face flame, and began to stammer. "My friends and I decided not to wear them, because we wanted to be more serious. But a lot of people at the march, men and women, had on these pink knitted hats with little points like kitty ears. They called them pussy hats."

"Why would they wear such a thing?" Mom asked.

"I know!" Bitsy cried, raising her hand like a student in school. "In the *New York Times* they said it was because you-know-who said he liked to grab them."

"Who's you-know-who?" asked Mom.

"Grab who?" asked Jane.

"Pussies!" crowed Margaret. She put her hand over her mouth and giggled.

Tittering ensued from one side of the room to the other. This was definitely not going the way I had predicted! I tried to interject. "I really think those hats were kind of a distraction—"

"I thought this was a political talk," said a woman in a wheelchair. "Can someone help me back to my room?" One of the other women got up to help her and the two of them left.

I drew a deep breath. If this were one of my freshman comp classes I could make them stay but obviously at age ninety people could do what they pleased.

"I just want to know why you'd go up there," said my mother.

"I went because I felt the need to be part of the energy of the movement," I said, in a rush of emotion, hoping that my mother would see. I realized, suddenly, that Mom had enjoyed the idea of organizing the talk but really had no idea what the march had been about. "I wanted to stand up for our democracy. I wanted to stand up for marginalized populations—"

"I don't understand," said my mother.

"I took a lot of pictures of the thousands of people on the mall. Would you like to see them?"

"Oh, yes!" said Bitsy.

I quickly found the pictures of the march on my tablet and held them up, showing the various clever signs that people had made, such as "I fight like a girl." One photo showed the mall itself with hordes of people like ants as far as the eye could see.

"Don't you have any pictures of the pussy hats?" demanded Margaret.

Why hadn't I prepared anything? I found a few of the hats in shots of the marchers crossing in front of the Washington Monument and walked around the semicircle, showing them to each of the women. On the end was a woman whose dementia was more advanced, but she looked at the screen as eagerly as everyone else.

"Why, even the men are wearing them!" Margaret said.

I thought I'd try again to redirect the conversation. "The atmosphere at the march was so inspiring—everyone was so friendly and upbeat and inclusive. When we got on the subway everyone cheered. There was such a tremendous sense of purpose to be at this peaceful march and to stand up for those populations that are being marginalized by this new agenda. There were *hundreds* of marches all over the world. It was so deeply meaningful to me to be a part of it. I don't know if I ever understood before how important it is to use your voice. I've gone all my life and never really used my voice. I've lived a safe life. I have never rocked the boat or disturbed the status quo. Going to this march made me wonder, 'What am I doing with my life?'"

I looked around at the women, feeling near tears that I'd blurted out such personal feelings.

My mother had fallen asleep.

The next week I went to pick Mom up to go to lunch and saw that she had an enormous bruise on the side of her face.

"Mom! What happened?"

"I fell last night. I tripped over my new walker." Mom grimaced.

I felt myself flush, feeling as if I was to blame. "Gosh, mom! We just can't win, can we? I need to take you right downstairs to the clinic."

"No, no!" my mother exclaimed. "It's nothing!"

"Oh, yes, we need to, you could have a concussion." I examined the knot on Mom's head, and the nurse's bandage on the skin tear on her leg she'd received from falling.

"Where is the alert to call the nurses that goes around your neck, Mom?" I scavenged through the cluster of Styrofoam cups on Mom's dresser until I found the coiled alert necklace.

"I took it off," my mother said dully. "I don't need to wear that thing."

"Yes, you do, Mom." Mom's resistance suddenly collapsed and

she obediently bowed her head for me to put on the necklace. She seemed to have slid back into the nearly catatonic state she'd been in the first few months after Dad's death.

I had a sinking feeling of helplessness as I helped Mom with her jacket and oriented her walker, and we headed down the hall toward the elevator. What could have caused this relapse?

"How's Bitsy?" I asked.

"Oh, they took her to health care. They cleared out her room. They stopped her chemo treatments. She's not allowed to have any visitors." My mother's face fell. "I don't think I'll ever see her again."

So that explained Mom's state of mind. I hugged her, feeling close to tears myself, thinking about Bitsy's enthusiasm for politics, the way she took such pride in reading the *New York Times*. I had become so fond of her in such a short time.

"She was my special friend," said Mom. "I miss her so much."

After a visit to the clinic, where the doctor examined the bump on Mom's head, and the nurse rebandaged her leg, I ordered a sandwich brought to Mom's room, rather than taking her out, and tucked her in for a nap. "I'll run some errands and come back in a little while," I said. While Mom napped, I headed to her old house to do some packing to get ready to put it on the market. Caitlin was coming to help me pack up in a few weeks, but I wanted to take care of the life-time of accumulated papers myself.

As I sat at my father's antique desk, I came upon his dog-eared paperback copy of *Europe on Five Dollars a Day*. My father's bold printing marked various pages. Memories of my family's trip to Europe flooded back. I had been ten years old, in fifth grade. I remembered my mother's thrill at visiting the Louvre, seeing the world-famous paintings in person, versus my father's scientific watch-checking approach—"No more than five minutes in this wing!" In Rome, my mother's awe in seeing Michelangelo's *Pieta*, and later, a clear memory of my mother crying, "But wait, this is where Keats lived!" as Dad insisted we had to catch a train. Our trip ended in England and Mom had been ecstatic about seeing Stratford-upon-Avon, and when we finally arrived for my father's physics conference in Manchester, my mother dissolved with sadness that it was all over.

I understood, in a rush, my mother's broken heart. So much was clear now, even Mom's complaints about the books I gave her. My mother's deteriorating vision and memory were making reading so difficult that almost every book seemed tedious. The pursuit of her lifelong passion had become impossible.

Almost in a daze, I locked the house and headed for the grocery store. I picked up a few items for my mother, and a cheery card and flowers for Bitsy. Inside the card, I wrote a warm note, ending it with "We need you in the resistance!" I dropped them off at the front desk in health care. Then I made a special trip to the library to check again for another Jack Reacher. One had been turned in! I felt ridiculously ecstatic, and delivered it to my mother, feeling a scratchiness in my throat as I passed Bitsy's empty room.

Later, as I hugged Mom goodbye, I glanced at the portrait of my gray-haired father in his blue shirt above the bed. Could I see the smile today? I was never completely sure. But I always at the last moment imagined that I did. The irony that I was seeking approval from a portrait I myself had painted did not escape me.

That night I dreamed that miraculously, Lee Child came to visit my mother. He was tall, pale, and rangy, almost skeletal, wore all black, and had to duck as he passed through the door to Mom's room. He sat on the couch next to my mother, practically folding himself, as if her room were a doll's house. He gave Mom a wry smile and cleared his throat. Then, in his clipped no-nonsense English accent, he opened and read the first chapter of his latest Jack Reacher novel to my mother.

"Your last one was a lot better," my mother said. "This one is rather tedious."

I felt the rising tension of powerlessness in dreams. How could my mother say that to him? Would he leave in an outraged huff?

"I know exactly what you mean," he said, patting my mother's knee, with a kind and patient smile.

In my dream, I wanted to hug him.

The Imaginary Husband

It's a crisp fall day when my husband Jeff and I pick up my ninety-year-old mother from the memory care unit at Salemtowne to take her to lunch. I have kept a routine of seeing her every week since my father died three years ago. We head to the Midtown Café, because there is room between the tables for her walker and the parking isn't difficult. The food is good, too, and the hostess always recognizes us and greets us warmly. A glass case in the back of the restaurant displays exotic desserts, and we usually treat Mom to one after lunch.

Mom likes to sit by the window. Our server, a young woman, approaches, and we place our orders, with Mom insisting on receiving her coffee right away. And could the server bring some crackers to munch on?

"Sure." Servers are almost always accommodating to Mom's sometimes high-maintenance requests. Mom is a tiny, frail woman with wavy silvery hair and nearly everyone finds her adorable. Except me. Sometimes Mom drives me crazy.

Mom orders pancakes for lunch. Jeff orders a hamburger and I ask for a chicken wrap.

"Lisa, I don't know if I should tell you this," she says as soon as the server has brought our drinks. "But I've remarried."

"Oh?" I nearly choke on my sip of water. "Really?"

"His name is Mr. Seig."

"That's a surprise! Does he live on your hall?" Jeff raises his eyebrows at me as he helps Mom with the cream in her coffee.

"No, he has a big house here in Winston and he comes to visit me. He eats with us sometimes. He's one of the wealthiest men in North Carolina. He owns a lot of property, and one of the reasons he married me is because he wants me to help him manage his property."

"Oh," I say. This has to be her imagination. "That's nice. So where did you get married?"

"He owns an island in the Caribbean and we went down there and got married on his yacht. The captain married us." Mom sips her coffee, not meeting our eyes.

"That sounds romantic. Why wasn't I on the guest list?" I ask. I can't help myself.

"Well," she says smoothly, "I tried to call you. I think you didn't pick up."

"Well, one day I'd like to meet him." There are times, I admit, when Mom calls and I don't pick up. She calls me about five times a day, forgetting that she's already called.

"Well, I'd like you to meet him, too. He's ninety-three. He is always sending me these beautiful dresses to wear and I tell him I don't have anywhere to wear them. I told him I was only marrying him for his money and he said, 'Oh, that's all right.'" Mom finds this amusing and laughs. Mom taught in the Forsyth County Schools for more than thirty years. She and my dad lived frugally, valued scholarship and integrity. She shopped at TJMaxx. To hear her saying these things is strange to me. I never thought she cared that much about money.

But I smile, nod, and take another careful sip of my water. At that moment, the server brings our food.

"Mr. Seig is going to buy Salemtowne and turn it into a theme park," Mom adds, as Jeff cuts up her pancakes for her. "And he's married me to help him manage the project. He said he thought I was the only one who could do it."

Jeff and I exchange glances and smile. The idea of turning a retirement center into a theme park strikes me as hilariously funny but I don't dare laugh. As we continue with our meal, Jeff and I try to bring Mom up to date on our daughters' lives, but Mom has other worries.

"Mr. Seig is keeping an eye out for that ring of clothing thieves," she says.

"Clothing thieves?" Jeff asks.

"Yes, there is a whole ring of thieves that have been stealing clothes from the people on my hall. I've called the police and the last I heard they had been apprehended."

"Well, Mom, if they've been apprehended then it's nothing to worry about."

"Well, people are still stealing my clothes, Lisa."

"I think sometimes the staff get people's clothes mixed up, that's all."

Jeff takes the check and goes to pay the bill and get us a dessert.

"I don't know why I didn't show you all those puppies that are living under my bed," Mom says. "The mother dog is so loyal to me. She's had three litters now. The man across the hall sold the first litter for ten dollars each."

"Maybe I can see them when we get back to the room," I reassure her.

"Did I tell you I've just gotten back from Moscow? There have been several art heists and I've been recruited by the FBI to recover the art."

"That sounds amazing, Mom. I'd love to hear more."

"Here you go, Mitzi." Jeff returns with a piece of chocolate pie, and then helps Mom divide it for the three of us. Mom waves down the server to bring each of us a plate. This is one of the things that drives me crazy. Mom's Southern propriety. When Jeff and the girls and I share a dessert we just put the plate in the middle of the table and take turns with our forks. All these dishes create more work for the server and more to wash. But even as I think about it, I realize it's petty, and tell myself to let it go. Mom loves sweets and usually eats more dessert than she eats of her lunch.

When we're finished, Jeff goes to get the car while I bring over her walker and help Mom out of her chair. As we're leaving an elderly gentleman using a walker takes a look at Mom, and says, "Hey there, pretty lady." The middle-aged woman with him scolds him. "Dad, are you flirting again?" The man winks at Mom and she absolutely beams. I remind myself to tell Jeff about this. He knows how much she values male attention. It's a reminder that, no matter how hard I try, because I'm female, I will always fall short in her eyes.

Our routine after lunch is to drive Mom around Wake Forest to see the campus, and then down Faculty Drive, our old street, where Mom and Dad lived since 1961. The new owners of the house fell in love with it; they had been looking for years for a mid-century modern with original fixtures. I was able to tour it once they'd reno-vated and it looked spectacular. I was delighted that the house was so loved. Mom wouldn't go in though; she sat in the car in the driveway.

Next, we take Mom to visit Dad's grave, and she continues with her stories as we wind in our car down the paved roads between the headstones, passing a green funeral tent, with a crew in muddy overalls digging beside it.

When we stop at Dad's gravestone, Mom, tired, stays in the car, and Jeff and I walk over and stand by the grave, arms around each other, remembering Dad. We brush colorful fall leaves from the flat stone. Below his name is carved, "Lieutenant J.G., World War II, Professor of Physics, Wake Forest University." Mom was so proud of the man Dad was and all he accomplished. We all were. Mom and Dad were inseparable for their last decade, and I have now realized that one reason for that was they both had dementia and were covering for each other. While Jeff and I stand there, I have the same recurring thought as always: that the leaves of the oak tree beside Dad's grave will move in the breeze, indicating that Dad knows I am here and is greeting me. I wait for them to move, holding my breath. And a breeze stirs and they shiver, a few bright leaves falling into the grass. I let out my breath and, as always, ask Dad for his help. Am I doing the right thing in the way I'm caring for Mom? Should I be keeping her in my house? I know I couldn't manage it but I still feel guilty. I want Dad to approve of what I'm doing.

"One thing I have found out about Mr. Seig was that I was married to him before I married your father," Mom says as soon as we get back in the car. "And I had a son by him."

"You were?" I ask. "You did?"

"Yes. I had gotten pregnant out of wedlock and his mother took that child from me and I was not able to raise him. Well, that son is grown now and he's being given an award and Mr. Seig sent over a beautiful dress for me to wear to the awards ceremony. And I said that I shouldn't go to the awards ceremony, that the mother who raised him should go. And I told Mr. Seig that he should give that dress to her. He didn't like that."

I am not sure how to answer, but I'm thinking that worrying about this child she never knew could create anxiety.

"Mom, Dad was the first person you ever married. And you were married to him for sixty-four years. You were not pregnant out of wedlock. You never married anyone else. You never had to give away a baby. You're imagining this."

"I am?" She looks at me wide-eyed.

"Yes. It's all in your imagination."

"I think you're wrong. You didn't know me then."

"I know that, but I know you were never married to anyone except Dad."

"Well." She looks confused and doubtful. "I hope you're right."

We take Mom back to her room and she is tired so she gets into bed for a nap. The staff has been trying to get her up to join in more activities on the unit but she remains uninterested. The only activity that has interested her so far was an Elvis impersonator and she talked about him for weeks.

Jeff leaves to go get her a Coke and she leans toward me and takes my hand.

"I want to die," she says. "Ever since Dad has been gone I don't have anything to live for. I just want to die."

"I know you do, Mom," I say. "I understand. But I don't know what to tell you. I guess you just have to hang in there." I could say that I love her and I don't want her to die. But I don't know if that's the right thing or not. So I just lean over and kiss her forehead, as if she is my child.

"Where does she get this stuff?" Jeff asks as we drive home. "It's almost like she's been watching some movie and incorporated part of the movie into her life."

"I know! Turning Salemtowne into a theme park!"

Jeff and I both allow ourselves to laugh at it now, and we joke about wild wheelchair rides and elderly cartoon characters and candy-coated pills.

"I never knew she had such a vivid imagination," I add. "When we were growing up she always seemed so sensible and down-to-earth. You're really good with her," I add, reaching over to place my hand over his. "Thank you for helping me take care of her." It touches me to watch him help her. His soft-heartedness is so endearing.

"You're welcome," he says. "She needs somebody."

Two or three days later Mom calls me. My feelings about her calls have changed—I just feel happy she can still remember the number. She never learned to use a computer or smartphone and sometimes I wonder if her dementia might have started much earlier than we originally thought. She is beginning to have trouble with the TV remote, and I'm worried that the phone might be next.

"I hate to have to tell you this," she says now, "but you know that I married that Mr. Cleary."

"I thought his name was Mr. Seig."

"Oh, well, he goes by both names," she answers smooth as silk. "Anyway, I believe that Mr. Cleary has died. I heard that they are sending a car for me to go to the funeral. But I don't know what to wear."

"You don't have to worry about going to a funeral, Mom," I assure her.

"The people that work for him don't want me to inherit any money from him. You know that he was the wealthiest man in North Carolina. I think that they might be trying to kill me."

Shock runs through my system. Does she truly think that? How awful that must be for her. "No one is trying to kill you, Mom. You're safe and no one is going to hurt you."

"I just think you're naïve, Lisa." She draws a deep breath. "You just don't know."

I spend the better part of a half an hour reassuring her that no one is trying to kill her and she doesn't need to go to a funeral today. Finally, we hang up. I am concerned, though, and I call the nurse on staff to see if she will go check on her. But then Mom calls me back a few minutes later.

"Mr. Seig had word sent to me that I was not to come to the funeral," she tells me. "It's because his family and the people who work for him don't want me to inherit any of his money. I think they're trying to kill me. There is money in my closet that they are trying to get."

"You're safe, Mom. You don't have to worry. There's no money in your closet."

"How do you know that?"

"I just know. Go look in your closet. You won't find any money."

"All right, I'll go look. Hold on just a minute." There is a sound of the phone being set down and I wait for a long time while she gets her walker and then shuffles over to her closet to inspect it. While she is gone I hear the closet door open and close and at last she comes back.

"Well, I was sure I had seen a bag with money before. Maybe someone already came and took it."

"You're completely safe, Mom. There was never a bag of money in your closet."

After ten more minutes of reassurances, we finally hang up.

The next week, Jeff has to work and so it's just Mom and me on our way to lunch at the Midtown Café when Mom says, "Well, you know, when that Mr. Seig married me, I told him I was only marrying him for his money, and he said, 'That's all right.'" She laughs at her joke. "But really, as I got to know him, he was such a sweet and caring man that I came to love him. But now he's died and I'm all alone again."

I wrack my brain for the right response. Should I correct her? Should I go along? Finally I just decide to comfort her.

"I know, Mom," I say, and squeeze her hand. "I'm so sorry."

Gladiator

The call comes midafternoon.

"Your mother has fallen again," says the nurse from Mom's memory care facility. "Her lacerations are so bad we need to send her to the hospital for stitches."

I jump in the car for the ninety-minute drive. How many times have I done this over the past four years? Fifteen? Twenty? As Mom's mental and physical faculties have diminished, her falls have become more frequent. She has been told a thousand times not to get out of the bed without calling the nurse, but she can't remember. And so she tries to get up, and she falls.

I arrive at the ER entrance just as EMTs are sliding a gurney from the back of an ambulance. I glimpse a frail frame under a tight white blanket. Before I see her shrunken face or her flyaway white hair I know it's my ninety-two-year-old mother.

"Hi, Mom!" I say, placing my hand on the blanket over her ankle.

"What are *you* doing here?" Mom gives me a puzzled look.

"To keep you company at the hospital," I say.

"We had some bandaging to do," says one EMT, as I follow them into the ER. "She has some pretty bad gashes."

"These two young men taking care of me are darling," Mom tells me.

"I'm so glad." She has always loved the attention of men.

The doctor arrives quickly, since Mom came by ambulance. When he peels back the bandages I nearly cry out with shock. Mom's wounds are as big as raw steaks and just as bloody. Her skin is so fragile. How will they repair these gaping wounds?

"Hmmm," says the doctor.

"Where are you from and where did you go to medical school?" my mother demands.

The doctor gamely gives Mom his background as he gently examines the wounds. "There is no way I can repair these," he finally says. "No stitch would hold with her fragile skin. They used steri-strips at the home and I can just add a few more. We can just hope for the best. But first I'll send out for some X-rays to make sure nothing is broken."

There was a time when I would have been terrified. I've been with Mom to the hospital so many times before over the past four years, though, that I must admit that I am used to this.

"What are *you* doing here?" Mom asks again, glaring at me.

"I'm just here to keep you company here in the hospital, Mom."

"That young doctor was pretty nice-looking."

I have to laugh. "Is that why you keep coming here, Mom? To hang out with these young doctors?"

While we are waiting for the results from Mom's X-rays we watch *Gladiator*, with Russell Crowe, on mute, on the TV in her cubicle.

Though we can't hear the dialogue, we watch the emperor, played by Joaquin Phoenix, release tigers into the arena, intending for them to kill Russell Crowe. The emperor's wife, from the expression on her face, is clearly in love with Russell Crowe instead of the emperor. Miraculously, Russell Crowe kills all of the tigers. Again and again, out in the arena, he lives to fight again.

It's hours past dinner and I can tell Mom is hungry. I grab my purse. "I'm going to get you some food, Mom. I'll be back in just a few minutes. Do not try to get up from this bed—you could fall. Do not, I repeat, do not get up." In spite of the fact that I sprint to the cafeteria, grab the first sandwich I see, and run back, by the time I return she is halfway off the bed, about to fall, and I have to call for help. Fortunately a nurse comes running and helps me wrestle her back onto the gurney.

Once she has eaten a few bites of the sandwich Mom cocks an eye at me. "What are *you* doing here?" she says.

Why does she keep asking me this? Is it possible that, for the first time, Mom doesn't know who I am? I've heard friends with parents with dementia tell stories about this seminal moment, about the abject feeling of loss when they realize their own parent does not know them. Yet with Mom this has been such a long journey that I feel like I need to be matter-of-fact about it.

Finally the results of the X-rays come back and there are no broken bones and we have the green light to clean and bandage the wounds. As the doctor gingerly pours saline solution onto Mom's lacerations, I hold her hand tightly but still she cries from the pain.

"We've been watching *Gladiator* on mute," I say to the doctor as he works.

"Yes. I've seen it at least a dozen times." He gently pulls the torn skin back into place over Mom's leg.

"So, since I can't hear the dialogue, is this the climax? The battle between Russell Crowe and the emperor?"

"Yes. But the emperor gave Russell Crowe a fatal wound before the fight." The doctor painstakingly attaches tiny steri-strips around the edges of the wound. "He stabbed him in the liver so he bleeds internally. And so Russell Crowe kills the emperor, but then Russell Crowe dies too."

The doctor stands up and removes his gloves. He looks exhausted. "That's the best I can do. They need to change these bandages every single day at the home."

"I'll be sure to tell them."

"You should not try to put your mother in your car with these wounds," he says. "Have the ambulance take her. I'll call them now."

Mom and I wait an hour for the ambulance. *Gladiator* ends, Russell Crowe dies, and the credits run.

At last the EMTs arrive, two young women amazingly cheerful to be still at work at this hour. As they wheel Mom by me on the way out, she hands me something small. "I found this in my mouth," she says.

I open my hand. It's one of her teeth. Her body is literally falling apart. "Oh, my gosh, what should I do with this?"

"Tooth fairy?" suggests one of the EMTs.

We all collapse with laughter, laughter so bursting and frenetic it hurts my stomach.

"Mom, I guess we need to go to the dentist."

"Oh, that dentist," she says. "He's so good-looking he'll take your breath away."

I follow the ambulance back to the retirement center where my mother stays. The staff members come to get her settled in her bed. I pull her blankets up around her shoulders the way she likes them and lean down and kiss her cheek.

"I'm glad you came," Mom says. "What would I do without you?"

"Oh, you'd do fine, Mom." I realize my eyes are misting. She does still know me, at least right now. And I guess I do care—more, much more—than I thought.

Oh, I Wish I Could Tell You

Mom, do you remember our dog Candi, the little brown feist? She always played second fiddle to our male dog, Calvin. He ate her food, he stole the lion's share of the attention, he was the first to bark and race to the front door if someone rang the doorbell. After he died, Jeff and I thought Candi would revel in being the only dog. We thought she would enjoy her time in the spotlight.

We were wrong.

For a month after Calvin died of leukemia, Candi acted heartbroken. She retreated to her bed with no appetite. One day we carried her outside and when Jeff put her on the ground, she fell over onto her side. She was barely able to walk for several days and my veterinarian husband determined she must have suffered a stroke. She barked constantly when Calvin was around, but since Calvin died, she has never barked again.

Candi used to trot around the small circular park in front of our house, her ears perked up, enthusiastically sniffing all the smells from the other dogs. After Calvin died she shuffled along with her head down. Sometimes she'd stop and just stand there for a long moment, with no will to go farther.

When you used to come to visit us after Dad died, we would walk with you around that little park, too, remember, Mom? Our walks were slow, because you were weak. You used a gnarled walking stick that Dad had made for you from the branch of a tree. Gradually, you needed a walker, and eventually, you couldn't make it all the way around the park. We'd go about a third of the way around and have to turn back. Eventually, you became so feeble that you couldn't do that little walk at all.

You and Dad were married for sixty-four years. You were truly constant companions. You went everywhere together. Church, plays, doctor appointments, the grocery store. You kept a patter of conversation going all the time. There was such a strong connection between you, and you were such long-standing companions for each other, I couldn't imagine either of you alone. Dad was a fairly serious person and you gave him joy. You were vivacious; you loved music, loved to dance, loved being around people and having fun.

And then Dad died. You sank into despair. You had difficulty dressing yourself. You had no appetite and quickly lost fifteen pounds. You had a series of mini-strokes. Your memory suffered and while there may have been an element of dementia, I believe much of what happened to you was supreme grief.

Sometimes I would be able to see a glimmer of your previous joy in life. One day, for example, you told me that an Elvis impersonator came to your memory care unit and you seemed to enjoy that as much as anything you'd experienced since Dad passed away. You falsely remembered that I was a big Elvis fan. I was more of a John Lennon sort of girl but you were so excited I hated to correct you.

At the time, I thought about our little dog, Candi, slowly making her way around the little park, bit by bit regaining her strength and one day making it all the way around, tentatively sniffing here and there. I hoped that maybe one day soon we could bring you back and you would be able to make that walk around the park too.

But you never made it around the little park again. One day last winter, when I had visited you and stood in the doorway, ready to go, you said, from the bed, "Lisa, I'm going to die soon. I don't want to stay here anymore."

I went back into your room and sat in the chair by your bed. I took your hand.

I didn't want to pretend; we both knew you were close to death. Your quality of life was very poor; it consisted of lying in the bed and struggling to get to the bathroom and back.

"Your hand is cold." You said and pulled your hand away. That hurt my feelings. I felt a sinking sadness not to be able to offer you physical comfort, even though it was you who was dying.

"I feel like I never recovered from your Dad's death," you said.

"I know what you mean." It was true. Your eyelids, usually closed, were translucent. I wondered if you were dreaming, or if some part of you had already left this world.

"Are you scared?"

"No." You shook your head, your eyes still closed.

"Maybe you'll be able to be with Dad again." I felt the need to say something hopeful.

"Oh, I don't believe in any of that. I don't believe in life after death any longer. I don't even know if I believe in God."

That stunned me. You were such a devout young woman, and our family attended the Methodist Church faithfully as I was growing up. Even though I knew your beliefs evolved as you aged, as mine have, I was still shocked to hear you say this. Did I believe you might see Dad again? I wasn't sure now what I believed any longer. We talked for a few more minutes, then I kissed you on the forehead and drove home, crying part of the way.

Three days after that conversation, the nurse on your hall called me. "I'm so sorry to tell you this. Your mother has passed away."

I stared across our kitchen. I wasn't surprised. You had told me. I heaved a sigh, and tears slid silently down my cheeks. In your last weeks, you had been half in this world, half on the other side. Yet, even though we'd had sixty-five years to tell each other what we thought, wasn't there more, so much more, to say?

"We don't understand it," the nurse said. "She had a good morning. She went to lunch with the group today, which she hadn't felt up to doing in a while. Then she came back to her room to take a nap and when we came in later she had passed."

Could I admit that my strongest emotion was relief? You were so happy with my father and so very lost without him. So rudderless. Without him, your life seemed to have no purpose. And as hard as I tried, I couldn't make anything better for you.

When I was younger, I used to want to tell you everything that ever happened to me. It almost didn't seem as though it had happened until I'd told you about it. Even the smallest thing, like who said hello to me in the high school hallway. And I knew that you cared about everything that happened to me in a way that almost no one else has, except now my husband. You shared my triumphs, my griefs, my fears, my funny moments. I think of you almost every day now, usually to think, "Oh, I wish I could tell Mom that."

You have been gone now for over a year, and, ironically, Candi is still with us. She's eighteen. She has somewhat recovered from her stroke and on some days is downright bouncy. She has milky, marble-like cataracts in both eyes and sometimes walks into walls. She wears diapers now; we call them her "fancy pants." They come with cheerful little patterns on them, like duckies and flamingos.

There are some days when she can still make it around the little park in front of our house, but most days we have to turn back or pick her up halfway around. She still stops in the middle of the sidewalk and stands with her head down, with no will to go on. Sometimes when she's lying in her bed, sleeping, I watch her for a long moment to make sure she's still breathing.

She is a prickly little dog who doesn't like to be held or petted. The other night she leaned against me as I held her in my lap for a short time and at one point she turned and looked at me. Just as I settled in to snuggle with her and show her my love, she jumped down. I thought of you.

III

The Ruby Mirror

An Old Couch, Two Chairs, and Covid

In our first year of marriage, thirty-five years ago, my husband and I acquired a sectional couch with a subtle beige-and-white pattern. Don't ask me why I thought a white background was a sensible choice in a house with five cats. I was young. It was expensive. I thought it looked elegant.

Once our oldest daughter was born, this couch was where everyone sat to take pictures. We have multiple photos of my parents, Jeff's parents, and our friends sitting on this couch holding Caitlin as an infant and toddler, and then, a few years later, holding our younger daughter, Kelsey. As the girls grew, we sat on that couch to listen while they practiced piano. My book group sat there for book discussions.

Over the years, I vacuumed and spot-cleaned that couch, washed the pillows repeatedly, and finally had it re-covered. It moved with us four times, from a place of honor in our first living room to being hidden upstairs in my office in our present home. It went from being the hallowed spot for family photos to a repository for books and manuscripts and a place for our (now one) cat to sleep and sharpen his claws.

A few weeks ago, I admitted it was time for the couch to go. Thirty-five years is an exceptionally long life for a couch. I ordered two sleek recliners to replace it.

And then the difficulties began.

One day, two giant boxes appeared via "contact free delivery" on our front porch. Jeff and I struggled to get them in the door.

"We're weaklings," he said. "I'm not sure we can move these bad boys."

"Bad boys?" I teased my husband. This was the term he always used with things that were really heavy.

By the time we had them inside we were exhausted and Jeff had nearly thrown his back out.

"Let's worry about these bad boys tomorrow," I suggested.

The following day Jeff and I used all the strength we had to pull the two recliners out of the boxes. Finally, huffing and puffing, we dragged them out and managed to dislodge the Styrofoam packing.

"The comments on the web page said assembly was simple," I assured Jeff.

He gave me a shocked look. "Assembly?"

The assembly video had suspiciously soothing music playing in the background. The guy looked unruffled, never breaking a sweat as he attached the seat to the back. That morning, we watched it 1,239 times.

We were both sweaty and uttering words we hadn't used since our twenties.

Finally, both chairs sat in the front hall, assembled. And Jeff and I were, miraculously, still alive and married.

"We should have carried the pieces of the chairs upstairs before we assembled them," I told Jeff. "Now these bad boys are too heavy for us to carry."

"Are you making fun of me calling these bad boys?" Jeff asked.

"Yes," I said.

"Well, yeah," Jeff admitted. "We should have. But we didn't. What about these boxes?"

"We'll worry about them tomorrow."

The following day, we broke down the boxes, loaded them in the car and Jeff took them to the recycling center. Back home, he said he had only a minor conflict with the recycling employees who wanted to fine him fifty dollars for putting the Styrofoam in the wrong bin, but was finally able to correctly dispose of it.

Meanwhile, I called some charities to see if they'd come get the couch. Because of Covid, several weren't picking up donations. The ones that were still picking up asked people to bring items out on their front porch so the volunteers wouldn't have to come into the house.

How to get the couch down the stairs and out onto our porch?

I called our daughter, Kelsey, and offered dinner if she and her boyfriend Seph would come help us. She said they'd be delighted.

A few days later, Kelsey and Seph showed up looking confident. We had sadly only seen them a few times since the onset of Covid.

"We just need to move these bad boys upstairs," Jeff said.

"Bad boys, Dad?" Kelsey said, and we all erupted in laughter.

"Easy peasy," said Seph.

And for them, it was. They helped Jeff carry the new chairs upstairs, and with much teamwork, maneuvered the couch down and onto the porch. We were insanely grateful, since we'd had the chairs sitting in our front hall for four days. Ah, youth.

The following day, the charity truck pulled up and my husband joyfully greeted the volunteers. However, the moment they stepped on the porch, they shook their heads.

"This couch is too old," said a white-haired volunteer. "We can't put this out on our floor. We can't take this."

"But do you know how much work it was to get this couch out here?" Jeff protested. "We can't take it back inside by ourselves."

The volunteers were unsympathetic. They swung back into their truck, leaving the couch sitting on our porch.

"What do they mean, 'it's too old?' It wasn't too old for us!" I complained. "Doesn't everyone keep couches for thirty-five years?"

We scrambled to find another charity that might come. After a slew of phone calls, we finally found one that would come the next day.

I didn't sleep well that night. I dreamed that the second charity also refused to take the couch. Then had a terrifying nightmare about being called to account before the homeowners' association. Jeff told me I worried too much.

That next morning Jeff and I paced the kitchen after breakfast.

"Take some twenties in your pocket when you go out there," I suggested. "If they refuse to take it, you can offer to pay them to take it to the dump."

"Good idea," Jeff said.

At last the moment of truth arrived as the truck pulled up in front of our house. The volunteers greeted Jeff by giving him the printed receipt for our donation. My heart was in my throat. Miraculously, the volunteers tossed the couch and its faded pillows into the back of the truck and pulled down the gate. Jeff handed them a tip to seal the deal. They seemed pleased. Then he and I stood breathlessly inside the front door, looking out, until the truck pulled away.

"They took it! They took it!" We danced around in our front hall, dizzy with relief.

Maybe they did take it to the dump. Maybe someone who recovers couches took a look and decided it had good bones. At any rate, our old couch, home to posed photos, kissing sessions, arguments, wrestling matches, piano practice sessions, discussions about books, boyfriends, and current events, foot rubs, piles of manuscripts, and many generations of cats, had transitioned to a new existence. It felt bittersweet. The end of an era.

We went upstairs and lowered our old bodies into our new chairs.

"This chair is so comfortable, I don't think I can get up," Jeff said.

"These bad boys are so nice, we can keep them for at least thirty-five years," I added. And I reflected with gratitude over the years of our marriage, our family, and the health and happiness we've had.

Don't Give Up

(Adapted from a Closing Keynote speech given at the 2019 Society of Children's Book Writers and Illustrators conference)

Writing has been an exhilarating and painful journey for me, the source of some of my life's highest highs and lowest lows. I have terrible doubts every day about whether I have what it takes, about whether I have enough talent, about whether I will ever write anything that is really, really good. And it's a tough business. When you write a piece, it might get rejected dozens of times before someone accepts it. You might get rejected by dozens of agents before one will take you on. Once a publisher actually buys your book, your editor is going to look at the manuscript and want you to make changes that are sometimes massive. So, there's more revision. After the book comes out, then you have to worry about whether the reviews are any good. You have to worry about the sales numbers and whether anybody actually reads what it is you've written. The sheer impossibility of some of these odds can be paralyzing. This is not a business for the faint of heart.

After my first and second books, *Eleanor Hill* and *Princesses of Atlantis*, had been published, and *Eleanor Hill* had won an award, I sent Carus, my publisher, my third novel, *Summer of the Wolves*. It was about two stepsisters and the complicated relationships of young girls. I'd written it with a great deal of passion and sent it off, brimming with confidence about the power of the story.

My publisher rejected it.

I felt like I'd been punched in the gut. I cried for three days. I walked around like a zombie. Food had no taste. I became like a walking ghost to my husband and snapped at my children.

I sent it to two or three other publishers. They rejected it too. *Wow*, I thought. *This novel must be really bad.* My thoughts twisted around themselves like the true paranoiac that I am. Obviously, I didn't really know anything about writing. Probably no one would ever want to read anything else I ever wrote again. I guess this was my first dark night of the soul. I put the novel away.

But after a while, I couldn't stop writing, so I signed up for a writing workshop. And there I met the two people who would become my writers' group for many years. I was so ashamed that my third novel had been rejected that I didn't even tell them I had already published two novels. I went incognito. I passed myself off as a new writer.

With them, and another writing group, I wrote another novel. I had no success with that one, either.

At last, I enrolled in a master of fine arts program. And, for a few years, I focused on my craft and on making more connections with other writers. During that time, I won an award for one of my short stories and published a few more.

After being in the MFA program, I managed to find an agent and sold another novel, *Write Before Your Eyes*, to Delacorte. It was a tribute to books I'd loved during my childhood. The book was about a quiet girl who finds a magic journal, and everything she writes in it comes true. It was a joy to write.

And after that book came out, my agent said, "Do you have anything else?" And yes, I did—*Summer of the Wolves*, the story that had been rejected four years before and broken my heart. "Send it to me," she said. So I did. And after a few weeks, she called me and said, "What if you were to rewrite this in first person?" It had been written in two voices in third. That was a fair amount of work. But I am always willing to try something. So I agreed and rewrote the whole novel in first person. About four months later, I sent it back to her. Probably two months later, she wrote to tell me she'd sold it and that the editors also wanted three more books with those same two characters. And once those were written, they asked me to write another one. I couldn't believe this was happening to me.

My entire career has been one example after another of "Don't give up." I am not a great talent, but I am a hard worker. I keep trying. Over the years, I've noticed that many successful writers are the ones who revised twenty-five times instead of just twice and sent to a hundred agents instead of twenty. I heard the stories about every editor in New York rejecting *A Wrinkle in Time*. About Kate DiCamillo's 470 rejection letters. I once heard Jane Yolen speak at a regional Society of Children's Book Writers and Illustrators meeting about her unpublished manuscripts. I was gobsmacked—Jane Yolen, the amazing and famous Jane Yolen, author of the riveting *Girl in a Cage*, with unpublished manuscripts? These authors inspire me.

One of my later novels was sent out by two agents and couldn't find a home. But I had learned from that first heart-breaking rejection, and I decided not to give up. I researched small presses, sent query letters, and found a lovely small press called Blue Crow Publishing that, after an R and R (revise and resubmit), published

One Week of You and also asked me to write a prequel novella, *One Week of the Heart*. For the last couple of years, I've been working on an adult historical fiction novel, something new for me. I've written it in third person, switched to first, then back to third. I tried it in chronological order, a dual timeline, and then back to chronological. And I have found a home for it!

I've published twelve novels but written fifteen. Will those other three ever see the light of day? I hope so. I keep working on them.

The Walkway to the Beach

Jeff and I found out about the walkway in the lawyer's office when we closed on the house.

"You have deeded access to a walkway to the beach across the street from your house, beside the yellow waterfront house," said the closing attorney, a casually-dressed guy with an alluring Southern accent.

"Oh, really?" I asked. "I assumed we had to walk the half block to the public walkway."

"No, your house, and your house only, has deeded private access to that walkway next to the yellow house. But it's only grandfathered once. If you sell the house, the deeded access disappears."

"There's no reason to worry about that." Jeff's face was flushed with excitement and joy. "We're never going to sell this house!"

On our way to our new house, keys in hand, Jeff was ebullient. "A deeded access! We didn't even know we had it!"

I had never seen him so happy. He had wanted a beach house for as long as I had known him. He had been a workaholic veterinarian for most of our marriage, dreaming of the time when he had more free time and could go to the beach.

A part of my soul was there, too. My maternal grandmother, whose father was a fisherman, grew up in Atlantic, on the North Carolina coast, and I had gone to Emerald Isle and other North

Carolina beaches every summer of my childhood.

Now, in our sixties, we finally had enough money for it and we'd done it. We'd bought a three-bedroom second-row beach cottage. It was old, and needed work, but it was a house at the beach.

At the beach, second-row dwellers are clearly second-class citizens. You can't hear the pounding of the surf from your bedroom window, you can't smell the fragrant ocean breeze, or see the dunes or the gorgeous sunrises right outside your living room. If you want to completely enjoy the fruits of this environment, you must somehow find a pathway to the beach. Our pathway was a miracle!

"We've earned it!" Jeff crowed. "We've worked all these years and now it's time to reap the benefits of all our hard work."

The moment we arrived at our house, we skipped across the street to the walkway, accessed by a creaky wooden gate with a latch, that allowed us to get to that spectacular beach. The wooden walkway stretched along beside the yellow house and over about forty yards of grassy protected dunes to the beach.

Everything was idyllic at first. Our old house had quirks, especially with the plumbing, and we both did dozens of projects to fix it up. Jeff worked on the beach walkway, too, pounding renegade nails and clearing the fast-growing vegetation that liked to wrap around your legs. Our children loved the house as well, and it was heavenly when both grown girls came down and we'd all be together at the beach house, with our four dogs and one courageous cat. We walked long distances on the beach, passing the black-and-gray striped Oak Island lighthouse, with mottled Old Baldy in the distance. We picked up dozens of perfect, paper-thin, ethereal angel wings, that seemed to symbolize the perfection of this place. We sat under an umbrella on the beach and joked, read books, and caught up with our daughters' young lives. At the house we gorged ourselves on seafood and low-country boils, played games that left us breathless with laughter, and put together puzzles.

Our family used the walkway nearly every day. We rented the house sometimes when we weren't there, and our rental company installed a sign saying "No Public Access: Private Walkway." The renters who stayed in the yellow waterfront house, who had their own side entrance to the walkway, were usually friendly as we walked back and forth to the beach. I have to be honest, I sometimes felt we were encroaching on their privacy, as we had to walk up their driveway to access the walkway, and the walkway was right next to their porch and swimming pool. But, I told myself, we did have deeded access. We had the right. Sometimes, though, if there was a particularly boisterous family at the yellow house, I would walk down to the public walkway to get to the beach just to avoid them. But I never admitted that to Jeff or our daughters.

Once or twice someone on the beach approached us and asked what house we were staying in. When we told them, they seemed satisfied. It gradually became clear, as we spent more time and got to know more people, that some of the permanent residents did a bit of freelance policing of the beach to make sure unauthorized people weren't using that walkway.

As time went on, we learned more. The builder of our house had originally owned three oceanfront lots in a row, and our house had been built on that first row in 1964. In 1992, the builder moved our house to its present second-row location, and built large rental houses on the three lots he owned on the front row. He lived in our house, and created the deeded access for himself, so that he could easily cross to the beach. In order to help sell the house when the time came, he had grandfathered the deeded access. To us.

Neither of our families have a history with limited access. We've never lived in gated communities. My parents came from modest means and decided not to join our town's country club, even though it was just across the street, for two reasons: First, they couldn't afford it; and second, on principle, because the golf team from the local college where Dad taught had been turned away when it had its first Black members. And Jeff's family, being Jewish, had been excluded from many of the Bethesda clubs when he was growing up, and also as a matter of principle, never joined any. Jeff and I once joined a golf club and later dropped out when we realized we didn't fit in. So, being on the other side of this issue was new to us.

Gradually, we became aware of just how coveted that walkway was. An acquaintance of ours texted and said, "Do you mind if I park in your driveway when you're not there and use your walk-way?" Then someone else asked. We always said, "Sure!"

Everything was fine until two things happened. First, the pandemic meant that Jeff and I were isolating at the beach more often. And second, the two elderly women who lived in the house next to us moved to a nursing home. They sold the house to a new owner who undertook massive renovations. The house had been modest before; once the renovations were complete, the house was gorgeous. While the new owners were renovating, we took them a bottle of wine and greeted them.

"So, how do you get to the beach?" the husband asked as we stood on their back deck overlooking the marsh, gleaming in the sunset.

"Well, you can use the public walkway," Jeff said.

"What about that walkway next to the yellow house, the one you use?"

"Well, that's a sticky wicket," Jeff said. "We have deeded access, but I don't believe any other houses have it. You could contact the owner of the yellow house. Maybe you could buy in?"

It was a very awkward conversation. However, that new owner began using the walkway anyway. We didn't know whether he'd talked to the owner of the yellow house or not. And the people who rented his newly renovated house also began using the walkway. Despite our clearly-worded sign.

Then came the long-awaited day when the owner of the yellow house came down, just for the day, to do some maintenance. Jeff made a point of accosting him while he was working on the yard, and told him the issues that had arisen with both the owners and renters of the house next to us using the walkway.

The owner of the yellow house seemed very annoyed and tired. He told Jeff he was thinking of putting his house on the market; his wife didn't like coming down with him, and he was worn out with beach house maintenance. "Besides, I don't really believe *you* have the right to use the walkway," he told Jeff.

"But we were told we had deeded access at the closing for our house several years ago," Jeff said, taken aback. "It's in our closing paperwork."

"That guy did not tell me he had grandfathered the access," the yellow house owner said sourly.

Jeff felt that they talked long enough for the owner to be convinced, but came home troubled.

The very next time we came down, a renter at the recently renovated house beside us came up to my husband and said, "Can we use your walkway?"

And when Jeff said, "Well, I paid for it, it's deeded, and I don't believe your house has deeded access," the renter responded, "Well, we've got our stuff down there already, we'll just leave it there today." But then they continued to use the walkway for the rest of their stay.

Jeff became irate. He watched them come and go on the walkway with growing fury.

"I'm getting a padlock for the gate," he said.

I wasn't sure how I felt. Sure, they were breaking the rules. We had paid for access and they hadn't. But they also had two small children who would have difficulties walking the half block to the public access.

When I texted our daughter to tell her how angry her father was, she responded, "Does he know there's a pandemic going on? Children being separated from their parents at our border? And a whole Black Lives Matter movement? Why is he getting so upset about a walkway?"

Marriage of course doesn't mean you agree about everything. I had often felt like an interloper on that pathway myself, despite the deeded access, and had chosen to walk down to the public pathway. I didn't think the new owners of the house next to us or their renters were right to use the pathway, but I told Jeff I also feared that any possibility of a cordial relationship with the owners would be forever destroyed if we put a padlock on the gate. Also, the beach wasn't crowded. It wasn't as though a few extra people were going to cause any discomfort for the rest of us.

"We don't really have the right to tell people whether or not they can use the walkway. I don't know if we have the right to put on a padlock," I told Jeff. "Wouldn't that right belong to the owner of the yellow house?"

"I'm putting on the padlock tomorrow," he said.

"I just don't want you to become obsessed with this," I pressed. "This house is your dream, everything is lovely and wonderful, why ruin it, why poison it, with worries about the walkway? Why not just let it go?" I said.

"We paid for this," Jeff said. "I can't let these people trample on what we worked so hard to earn."

Jeff got a padlock and put it on the gate. We barely spoke that afternoon. I was so mad I must have walked ten miles down the beach. The waves rushed over the sand, sparkling in the sunlight; the pelicans flew by, skimming the water's surface; the shells lay shining, and I barely noticed.

The next renters arrived at the house next door. They were carrying a baby and the mother was on crutches. And now there was a padlock on the gate to the walkway.

I felt horrible.

Much of the joy I had previously felt at being at our beach house seemed to be seeping away. I found myself watching the walkway, not for my own sake, but for the sake of my husband, whom I love, to see if unauthorized people were walking on it. I told myself, this is sick, this has to be put behind us.

The disillusioned owner of the yellow house did indeed sell his house, and I dreamed that night that the new owner moved the walkway to the back of the house so that it would be inaccessible to anyone, including us. I've also dreamed that someone cut our padlock with wire cutters and threw it into the dunes. The fears that arose in my dreams—that making an issue of the limited access to the walkway could actually reduce our own—eerily came to fruition.

The new yellow house owner decided that the owner of the newly renovated house could not use the walkway. He also pointed out that in our deed, members of our immediate family were permitted to use the walkway but our guests and renters were not.

Jeff called our closing lawyer and asked him about it. He examined our closing document, and, with slow deliberation, he told us that the new owner was right, that as the owners, we were the only ones allowed to use the walkway, no one else. "Hard to imagine anyone being so selfish. But that's the way it is."

For a while, I went down to the public access to get to the beach. For one thing, hilarious as though it may seem, I didn't seem to be able to unlock Jeff's padlock, even though I knew the combination. For whatever reason, it didn't work for me.

Only about a month later, the new owner in the renovated house next to us who had wanted to use the walkway, put his house on the market. We have no idea if losing access to the walkway was part of his reasoning or not. A week or so after that, Jeff went across the street and removed the padlock. We had no discussion about it.

With our long marriage, sometimes our disagreements end that way. The discussion has already been ample, and the issues possibly too painful and deeply felt to open the wounds and reexamine. Sometimes one of us will admit they are wrong and change their mind. My husband is such a dear and steadfast man, loving to me, our daughters and his family and friends, and my heart squeezes when I see him talking baby talk to our little dog as he walks her.

So now I take long walks on the beach, reveling in nature's beauty, grateful for the time we can spend here, and smiling at anyone who will meet my eye.

A Covid Micro-Wedding

Our daughter, Caitlin, had planned a traditional October wedding at a mountain winery. She and Josh, her fiancé, became swept up in the teamwork, enjoyment, and frustrations involved in choosing appetizers and flowers, writing and practicing toasts, and making playlists. Jeff, as in the movie *Father of the Bride*, was being dragged along with extreme reluctance.

"Why don't they just get married on the beach across from our beach house?" he would complain to me while we were reading before bed. "We love that place so much."

"The kids want the mountain winery," I said.

"But the beach would be perfect."

Then Covid hit.

We waited a few months, learning about the pandemic first on the news, and then knowing people who had contracted it. Jeff and I agreed that this was not the right time to have a big wedding. We had a phone call with Caitlin, and, in the end, she made the decision.

"Will I still be able to walk down the aisle with Dad?" She was crying.

"Of course," we said.

A few days later, after we'd called all the guests and vendors and delayed the big celebration for a year, Caitlin called me.

"I still want to get married on the original day. What about our beach house? Can Josh and I get married on the beach, with just a few people?"

"Sure!" I had to laugh, since this was what Jeff had been angling for all along. Thrilled, I quickly reserved our beach house for the original wedding weekend, since we sometimes rent it out. I began to feel an excitement about the intimacy of this micro-wedding that was different from the intimidation I had about the big celebration.

On our family text thread Caitlin texted her sister, Kelsey, about the new micro-wedding.

Will you be my maid of honor?

Of course!

Will you be my wedding photographer?

Sure!

Will you do my hair and makeup for the wedding?

Love to!

Will you be the officiant?

Caitlin, I am already hair and makeup, photographer, and maid of honor. I think I'm going to be too busy to be the officiant.

Okay, Mom, will you be my officiant?

I would be honored, I replied.

And so I became the officiant for my own daughter's wedding. No more could I contemplate standing by during the ceremony, reminiscing about Caitlin's childhood and delicately wiping tears from my cheeks. I was going to have to hold it together and make this thing happen.

It was ridiculously easy to get ordained online—literally all I had to do was type my name. I kept saying to myself, "Is this really legal?" I could hardly believe that it was. Then I ordered the needed materials—an instruction book, a letter declaring that I was in "good standing," and a few decorative (but not official) marriage certificates.

Caitlin and Josh went to the courthouse and got a real marriage certificate that all three of us would need to sign after the ceremony. Then I made three phone calls: one to a restaurant who could cater the dinner after the ceremony; one to a florist for a bouquet; and one to a baker for a cake.

Caitlin came to visit us the following weekend and we found a short white dress that was priced at 50 percent off, and Josh was elated to find Hawaiian shirts at 70 percent off at a department store. He bought them for himself, his father, his brother, Kelsey's boyfriend, and Jeff. No one worried about shoes since we were going to be barefoot.

In nine days, our micro-wedding was planned!

During the weeks before the micro-wedding, I did become a little worried that our wedding was so small that our "vendors" might forget us. When I called the florist the third time about the bouquet, he started laughing.

"Getting nervous?" he asked. "Don't worry, we've got you down."

Meanwhile, I spent several days working on the ceremony, using wording that I found in the instruction booklet and other sources online. Caitlin and Josh chose the wording for their vows and ring exchange, and also chose two readings—one humorous, the other serious. I added a prayer. When I practiced the ceremony, it lasted about seven minutes. I worried about the fact that I was incapable of getting through it without blubbering during the entire thing. I knew, from making presentations as a writer and a teacher, that the only way around was through. I would have to practice.

And so I did. I practiced the ceremony nearly every day for two weeks. Gradually the waterworks decreased to the point where I was only crying in one spot—the middle of the prayer. The prayer was one I love, which is used in both Christianity and Judaism, which fits since we're an interfaith family. "May the Lord bless you and keep you, may He make his face to shine upon you, may He lift up his countenance upon you, may He be gracious unto you, and give you peace." The part of about the Lord's face shining upon us touched me so deeply. I told myself if I could just get through that prayer I would be home free. I practiced more.

The day before the wedding, the kids arrived and our beach house was full, with six people and four dogs. We went for a walk on the beach and saw that two houses down from us, people were assembling a pergola, hanging lanterns, and setting out rows of white chairs.

"Are you having a wedding tonight?" Caitlin asked one of the guys setting up.

"No, tomorrow night."

"No kidding! We're having a wedding down here tomorrow night too. What time is yours?"

"Six thirty."

"Ours is at five thirty. Wow, what a relief they aren't at the same time!"

That night, we hosted all eleven wedding guests, including Josh's family. We made a Mediterranean chicken recipe for the eleven wedding guests (with left overs for the dogs) from the menu that

Caitlin had planned. Then Caitlin and Josh told the story of their first date, which was simply walking Caitlin's dog, Kinsey, on the greenway. And they told about the night they first knew they'd fallen in love, when Caitlin offered Josh a glass of water and then realized she was so happy in his company she danced across the room to give it to him. Caitlin was full of funny stories, and kept everyone laughing, and Josh's family, whom we had just met for the first time that night, stayed until almost midnight.

The morning of the wedding dawned sunny and bright. We were delighted, as rain had been predicted and we'd talked about moving the wedding inside. Jeff and I went to pick up the flowers and cake.

"Hi there, we're picking up the bouquet for my daughter's wedding," I said as the bell tinkled as we entered the florist shop.

The guy behind the counter gave me a completely blank look.

"I'm Lisa," I reminded him.

"I don't think I have any record of a bouquet for Lisa," he said.

My heart went to my throat and I broke out in a cold sweat.

He burst out laughing. "I'm just messing with you," he said. "Since you called so many times, you know. I've got it right here." And he produced a lovely arrangement of hydrangeas and sunflowers.

Weak in the knees, I took the bouquet and we loaded it into the car.

"That wasn't *that* funny," I told Jeff. We drove to the baker's shop.

"I'm here for my daughter's wedding cake," I said.

Again, the shop owner gave me a look of puzzlement. "I don't think—"

"I know, you're just messing with me," I laughed. "The chocolate one with the starfish and turtles?"

She put her hand on her hip and shook her head. "No, really, I don't remember having a wedding cake for today."

I thought I might wet my pants.

Then recognition dawned on her face. "Oh, you mean the little one?"

"Yes!"

"I have that right here in the refrigerator."

Again, while relief poured through me like water, she produced a beautiful little cake in white chocolate, decorated with starfish and turtles.

Jeff and I got the cake and flowers home and I set the table for eleven. I practiced the ceremony again, tried to think of something else I had to do and couldn't come up with anything. So, Caitlin and Kelsey and I sat on the back porch and gave each other pedicures and facials and chatted and laughed. I looked at my daughters' happy faces, with the beauty of the marsh surrounding us, and wished that I could capture and freeze this moment, this day, forever. Meanwhile, Josh went to have lunch with his brother, Shane. Jeff took a nap, and Kelsey's boyfriend, Seph, who was training for a marathon, went on a fifteen-mile run.

At last the time for the ceremony arrived. I watched, with tears in my eyes, as Kelsey braided and arranged her sister's hair. Then Kelsey took sweet and emotional photos of me helping Caitlin dress. Just seeing Caitlin in the white dress with the bouquet, with such joy and anticipation on her face, evoked so many emotions. Josh's family came, clad in their Hawaiian shirts. Kelsey, her camera in hand, sent Josh over to the walkway to the beach to stare dreamily out to sea while waiting for his "first look" at his bride. Then, at the house, we had a glass of champagne and Jeff gave a teary toast, saying what a fine man Josh was and how good he and Caitlin were together. And then we all traipsed to the beach, leaving our shoes on the walkway and sinking into the sand, still warm from the day's sun.

I stood with Josh and his family while Jeff escorted Caitlin across the sand, Kelsey shot photos, and Seph held up his phone and turned on Spotify to play the same song Jeff and I had walked down the aisle to—"Wild Theme" by Mark Knopfler. I had no idea they were planning to play that song, and under any other circumstances I would have absolutely bawled, but I had a job to do.

"We are gathered here today . . . " I began. And so the next seven minutes flew by in a flash. Jeff, who is a veterinarian, did a humorous reading called "Why Falling in Love is Like Owning a Dog" by a comic named Taylor Mali. Shane did a more serious reading about marriage written by the Dalai Lama called "Instructions for Life in the New Millenium." After all my practice, I cried anyway—during the prayer, of course, right when I was trying to talk about the Lord's face shining upon us. But somehow I held it together the rest of the way, through Caitlin and Josh's vows, and through the ring exchange, to "I now present you with the newly married couple, Mr. and Mrs. Josh and Caitlin Lindsey."

Josh swept Caitlin into his arms and kissed her. Everyone cheered.

Jeff cried. Caitlin and Josh cried. Josh's family cried. I think Kelsey was too busy.

We filed off the beach and along the walkway, and Caitlin called to the other people preparing for their wedding, "The beach is all yours!" They waved from under their pergola.

Our sweet neighbors, as we filed past on the walkway, cheered, called out "Congratulations!" and blew bubbles at us that danced through the air, whirling and catching rainbow colors in the waning sunlight.

Back at the house, we signed and witnessed the marriage certificate, drank some champagne to celebrate, and then Jeff and Seph went to the Italian restaurant to pick up dinner. Jeff came back with a frenzied story about how the person up front in the restaurant said she had no record of our order (seriously?) but at the last minute a woman swooped in from the back room with two enormous bags, saying, "Are you Kline?" One of Josh's relatives had graciously made a video of the ceremony that we all watched numerous times. Dinner was wonderful, and we told more stories and then cut and enjoyed the exquisite cake. Finally, we all sat in a circle around our neighbor's firepit playing games. Afterward, my normally introverted husband played guitar for nearly two hours. As the sweet and salty beach breeze swirled around us, I kept looking around the firelit circle at all the joyous faces, especially our beloved daughter and new son-in-law, and thinking, this simple little wedding has been perfect.

And, to top it all off, I'm still ordained.

The Trouble with Mating Season

I wasn't ready to go to the beach. We needed to deal with too many things. My husband's mother, who was having some issues with forgetfulness. Both of our daughters' weddings in one month—one delayed because of Covid, the other that evolved just because of love.

Jeff had also been having cluster headaches. These are called "suicide headaches" because they are so severe that people die by suicide rather than endure the pain. Jeff had tried many treatments—medications, a painful nerve block—and the headaches continued. Each evening, around eight o'clock, they arrived. The anticipatory anxiety was almost worse than the headaches. And I'd be putting cold compresses on his forehead in a dark bedroom. Should we drive four hours away from his neurologist?

And need I mention our decrepit eighteen-year-old dog who could not be left with anyone?

Should we really just leave this behind and go to the beach?

Besides, the forecast was terrible. Rain for the entire week.

"We're going," Jeff said.

And so, a few hours later we were in the car on the way down 74, with our ancient dog, Candi, and our cat, aptly-named Lionman, because of his routine sneaky bites. Most people leave their cats behind. My husband, the veterinarian, does not.

"Smell that air!" Jeff said as we crossed the bridge, rolling down the windows. "It just makes me relax."

The sun shone on the waving grasses and the gnarled yaupon trees did backbends over the road. The salty ocean breeze blew between us. The weather was gorgeous, in spite of the forecast.

It just made me more tense. All the trouble we were trying to leave behind!

Within the hour, Jeff was ready for the beach. After a bout with melanoma, he slathers himself with sunscreen every day.

"I'll get the bed and towels ready and meet you down there," I said. I needed to decompress. As I made our bed, I wondered, *What if Jeff's headaches don't ever stop?* The neurologist was so capable and conscientious, yet to our every question—"What causes these?" or "How long does it take for them to go away?"—he would answer, "We don't know." *And Candi.* She wore diapers, she could barely walk, she had terrible cataracts and got stuck in corners. We had to take her out over a dozen times a day. How long could this go on?

The weddings were the happy part. We were crazy about our sons-in-law-to-be and the planning had been a joy. Yet there were a few worries. What about inviting this person? What about replacing that vendor?

And above all, how could we help Jeff's sister, the major caretaker, with his mother? More caretaking was needed. More visits. More talks.

Making the bed, my mind went back over my years caring for my parents, who both had dementia. The last time I saw my father. I remembered holding my mother's hand the week before she died. I remember how she had never recovered from my father's death.

All of a sudden, out of nowhere, came a thought: *What would I do without Jeff?* That thought jolted me. I put down the pillowcase and stared out the window at the golden waning sun, stunned.

At that moment my phone sang with a text message.

There was an alligator in the water. People came running up to tell me because I was swimming.

An alligator, during mating season, had somehow ended up in the ocean—only a dozen feet from Jeff. Another beachgoer raced to the edge, yelling, "GET OUT OF THE WATER!"

Jeff scrambled for the shore with only seconds to spare. People ran down the beach, shouting at other swimmers, like a scene from *Jaws*.

He texted again.

That guy could have saved my life.

I shook as I read his text. Was it coincidence that I thought about losing him the very moment he was near the alligator? I am not a superstitious person but sometimes things like that make me pause.

Jeff came in, visibly shaken, pale. I gave him my usual kiss, no fanfare, yet my heart was pounding in my chest. On his phone, he showed me the twelve-foot alligator thrashing through the surf.

We ate dinner, discussing what might have happened to the alligator. Did Wildlife Control coax him back to the marsh? Did he ever find his elusive lady friend? Those things we'll never know.

Then we talked about brushes with death we'd had over our lives. Jeff's melanoma. A near car accident I once had. Then our conversation moved to the weddings. Caring for his mother. While we were talking, Lionman bit my leg. And then we retrieved Candi, stuck behind a door.

Life, glorious life, teems with trouble.

To our surprise, that night, Jeff did not have a headache.

Bringing Back Leo

Gommy's weekend caretaker was visiting her mother in Africa, and coverage was needed, so Jeff and I offered to drive up. We piled our sweet little fawn-colored chihuahua, Joni, into her pink carrier, because my veterinarian husband can't go anywhere without her, and headed up the road on the seven-hour trip from North Carolina to Maryland. Joni, like many rescue dogs, has been a challenge to house-train, and we were worried about how she'd do in the high-rise. We acknowledged the possibility that she might pee in the elevator, like last time.

My husband's mom was nicknamed "Gommy" by Rachel, her first grandchild, as a toddler, and that has become what literally everybody calls her. Gommy is ninety-six, living in a high-rise in Leisure World, an independent senior living community in Silver Spring, with her cat, Leo. Gommy always had a force-of-nature personality and she functioned perfectly and with great momentum and aplomb until she hit ninety-four. She lavished affection on her cat, she played mahjong, she visited friends, she snow-birded to Florida, cooked briskets and kugels, shopped at Home Goods and Macy's and TJMaxx, and gave all manner of instructions, such as always reminding us to shake the orange juice before pouring it, to her children and grandchildren. Then she had a few fender-benders and had to give up driving. And then she started to forget things.

Everyone in the family was so used to Gommy being in charge of everything that adjusting to this decline was a challenge for us all.

Jeff's sister Sheryl and her family have become the major caretakers. Granddaughter Michele, who lives nearby, visits frequently, is in charge of finances, and is in constant contact with Gommy about whatever she needs, from cat litter to bagels. Sheryl, and her husband Rick, who live about three hours away, bring food, arrange for caretakers, take her to doctor appointments, do her taxes, and field several evening calls per week from Gommy, begging them to come over. Sheryl has recently been researching a small assisted living facility closer to her house, where there is twenty-four-hour coverage, and she can visit Gommy more easily.

I did these same things for my mother before she passed away in late January of 2020, one month before Covid hit, so I know what it's like for Sheryl and her family. You become obsessed. Caring for this beloved person becomes your life.

We arrived around dinnertime on Friday night. I stood with Joni and our stuff by the front door of the high rise while Jeff went inside to get the luggage cart.

"Are you moving in?" asked an elderly gentleman passing by, eying our suitcases, Jeff's guitar, the dog carrier, our coolers, and the bag with dog supplies.

"Just visiting for the weekend," I said, with an embarrassed laugh, a little abashed at being mistaken for a resident, and also about all our stuff. We cannot pack light.

Lately, we usually don't tell Gommy that we're coming, since she gets anxious and confused. We just show up.

"I'm so surprised to see you!" Gommy exclaimed as we hugged her in the front hall of her apartment. Vera, her weekday caretaker, greeted us warmly. She helps Gommy dress, and Gommy was wearing her usual matching blue-green sweatsuit, with Velcro fasteners on her walking shoes, her short gray hair neatly combed and her hearing aid nestled in her ear. Her brown eyes, always so expressive behind her glasses, have uncertainty in them now.

Vera went home a few minutes after we arrived, promising to see us on Monday, and we made some pizza and a calzone for dinner. Leo, a beautiful long-haired ginger cat with golden eyes, hid the moment we arrived with Joni. Leo, who has lived with Gommy for about three years, has always been a one-person cat, affectionate with Gommy, but skittish and shy with everyone else. The family debated whether to get Gommy a cat at age ninety-three, but cats are such companions for her, and she has never been without one in her adult years. Before Leo, Gommy's feline companions were Suki, Puddin, Fella, Rusty, Smoky, Shayna, Little One, and Zack.

"How about some pizza, Mom?" Jeff asked.

"Oh, no, don't worry about me, you two eat. I've already eaten." This is what Gommy says at every meal. Jeff put a plate of pizza in front of her and she ate it with alacrity.

"Whose dog is this?" Gommy asked, as Joni circled the table, scouring the floor for dropped crumbs.

"That's Joni, our dog," I said.

We took a few more bites, and served Gommy some cantaloupe and pineapple.

"Whose dog is this?" Gommy asked us again. Watching Joni's antics made Gommy smile.

"Ours!"

Taking Joni for walks provided a comic break from the looming problem of Gommy's memory issues inside the apartment. Joni loved getting to meet and greet people in the elevator. Decked out in her pink sparkly collar, she might have been Elle Woods' dog in *Legally Blonde*.

Once outside the elevator, a dapper man in his seventies said to me, with an Inspector Clouseau fake French accent, "Does your dog bite?"

I had to laugh. "I wish my husband was here," I said. "He loves *The Pink Panther*." I could just imagine Jeff and this gentleman reciting the entire movie to each other.

Once Joni was walked, I asked Gommy if I could help her get ready for bed.

"No, no, I can do it myself," Gommy said, defensively. "I don't need any help."

About ten minutes later, I went to check on her, and found her looking for her pajamas among her winter outfits.

I found her pajamas, and she finally let me help put them on, as she petted Leo and called him "my sweet baby." I noticed that she never used my name, and suspected she didn't remember it. She seemed to think I was one of her caretakers.

Saturday morning, after breakfast, Jeff left to walk Joni, and Gommy leaned across the table toward me in a conspiratorial fashion. "Who is that man?"

I sat up a little straighter, surprised. I had figured Gommy might not remember me, but not Jeff. "That's your son, Jeff."

"My son? That big tall man is my son?" Gommy's eyes widened in disbelief. Jeff, for the record, is five feet nine. Not that big and tall.

"Yes."

"I named him Jeff?"

"Yes, Jeffrey Michael."

Was she being critical of her own choice? "Yes, a really nice name," I added. "I like it."

"And you're his wife."

"Yes."

"I can't imagine that I have a son." She shook her head, downcast. "This is terrible, not being able to remember."

"I know, Gommy, it must be very upsetting." My heart pounding, I rubbed the back of her hand. "But it's okay, we all love you very much. This happens to a lot of people.".

I decided not to mention it to Jeff. It would hurt his feelings. There were times when I suspected my parents didn't know me, in the last months of their lives, but, perhaps because they were in the academic world, where it was so important to be sharp, they didn't admit it. They fought valiantly to conceal their forgetfulness about how to get around the town they'd lived in for fifty years, and both confabulated and pretended to know who I was. Gommy, in her usual forthright fashion, is honest about not knowing.

Later that morning, Jeff decided to clip Leo's front claws, and we grabbed a broom and lay down on the floor to try to coax him out from under Gommy's bed. When he finally emerged, we had the first good look at him in months, and were shocked by his appearance. He was rail thin and his fur was horribly matted.

"He doesn't look good," I told Jeff.

"I'm going to take him for some bloodwork," Jeff agreed. A friend, Bob, who is also a veterinarian, has a clinic not far from Gommy's house, and Jeff took Leo there for an exam and bloodwork. He came back two hours later with a diagnosis: plasma cell gingivo-stomatitis-- an immune reaction that infects the gums so they turn flaming red. Poor Leo's gums and teeth probably hurt so badly he could barely eat. Jeff told me that the only treatment would be to remove the cat's rear teeth, a long and involved procedure. Jeff also detected a heart murmur.

As I was walking Joni that afternoon an elderly man, after petting her, authoritatively and at length told me the history of chihuahuas being trained as guard dogs for Toltec temples in South America, which is the source of the expression "ankle-biters."

"Fascinating!" I said. Fortunately, gentle Joni hasn't ever tried to bite anyone. She barely even barks.

"These guys are all trying to pick up a shiksa," Jeff joked when I returned to the apartment and told him about the "ankle-biter" line.

"No, I think they're trying to pick Joni up," I said.

Saturday night, after dinner, I talked with Gommy about the assisted living center Sheryl had picked out. She'd visited it once. I asked her how she felt about making a change, about moving to be closer to Sheryl.

"Who's Sheryl?"

I tried not to let my surprise show. It was somewhat understandable that she might forget Jeff, since she only saw him every three months or so. But Sheryl, who came almost every week and stayed several days? "She's your daughter. She's been taking such good care of you."

I moved on, showing her some pictures of the assisted living center: the sunny yellow walls, the views of the woods, the cute café tables. Gommy's reaction was surprising. "I could do with a change of scenery," she said. "Nothing is holding me here."

After that Gommy took out her hearing aid, declaring she didn't need help with her pajamas. A few minutes later she appeared in the doorway of her bedroom.

"Can you help me?" I helped find and put on the pajamas, and she went to bed. Jeff and I retreated to her extra bedroom, with single beds like on *The Dick Van Dyke Show*, to discuss what to do about Leo. Jeff sometimes squeezes onto the single bed with me for a few minutes to talk about the day.

We had a text thread conversation with the extended family and agreement came quickly. Gommy was no longer able to care for Leo, and we couldn't expect her caretakers to do it. Besides, the assisted living facility didn't even allow cats. It became clear that we would need to take Leo home with us, and after he recovered from the surgery, we'd have to find him a new home. We knew we couldn't handle Leo with Joni and our part-Siamese cat, Lionman, who opens doors, is a loudmouth, and a bit of a bully.

The next morning Jeff went into the kitchen early and started making coffee. Lying in the narrow bed, I overheard his conversation with his mother when she wandered into the kitchen.

"What is your profession?" Gommy asked.

"I'm a veterinarian." This question must have been painful for Jeff, as he had applied to many veterinary schools, and finally been accepted at Araneta University in the Philippines, to his parents' great joy, where he matriculated and lived for four years. His parents made sacrifices to pay for him to go there, lovingly sent care packages every few weeks, and lived in a state of worry whenever typhoons came through.

"And . . . who are you?"

"I'm your son, Ma. Jeff."

"You're my son? I can't remember my own son!" I wasn't in the room but I imagined that maybe she sat down at the kitchen table in distress, and Jeff, holding back tears, hugged her.

We had a sweet day after that, though. Michele came over and we sat and shared memories of when the grandchildren were young, the way Popeye, their grandfather, used to take them to movies and fall asleep; many years of Hanukkah and Passover celebrations; and trips to Florida with Gommy after Popeye died.

"Remember that apartment you had in Florida, Mom?"

"I don't remember Florida at all."

"I assure you, you had a wonderful time," I said, after a beat.

"Is this my apartment?"

"Yes."

"And you all are visiting me?"

"Yes, Ma."

After Michele left, we watched Bridesmaids, with Kristen Wiig and Melissa McCarthy, and laughed so hard we cried.

Walking Joni that afternoon, we encountered aggressive geese and bold deer, neither of which Joni had ever seen at home. She became so distracted that she forgot to pee and unfortunately, did it when she got back inside.

Later that night, after dinner, Gommy's hearing aid began giving off screeching sounds. We tried to call the audiologist, but it was Sunday, and the office was closed. We tried changing the battery, and changing the wax protector, but neither helped. We would have to wait until Monday. We took the hearing aid off and put it on the charger. But then we had to try to communicate with Gommy without it.

"Turn up the TV!"

Jeff turned it up to stadium volume. "How's that?"

"What?"

"I said, how's that?"

"What?"

Joni jumped on Gommy's lap. "Whose dog is this?"

"It's ours, Gommy."

"What?"

"Ours!" Our throats were sore from speaking so loudly, so we put the hearing aid back in, but then it started screeching again. Finally, in despair, after she agreed to let me help her with her pajamas, Gommy took out her hearing aid and went to bed.

Later that night, Jeff sneaked into Gommy's bedroom, to see if she was asleep. She was, with Leo curled across her chest.

"We'll take him back," Jeff said. "But you and I just can't take on another cat. We have to find a home for him."

The next morning, as soon as Vera arrived, we needed to leave. We piled our stuff on the luggage cart, and grabbed the broom to scare Leo from under the bed again.

"Mom, I have to take Leo with me," Jeff said. "He's very sick. I have to do surgery on him."

Gommy blinked. "So, I won't have a cat anymore?"

"It will take a while for him to recover from the surgery. He will stay with me. I'll take good care of him." We'd decided to be vague about not bringing him back.

"We'll send you pictures," I added.

"You will?"

"Yes."

"Good-bye, Leo." Gommy patted Leo on the head with her arthritic fingers. "You know," she said, "with my memory problems, I really can't take care of him very well anyway."

I wanted to cry. Gommy knew, even though we hadn't told her. She knew.

"Now, whose dog is that?" Gommy demanded. "Are you taking the dog too?"

"Yes, Ma, we're taking the dog too."

On the way home, Jeff said, jokingly, "Mom forgot about me. Maybe she'll forget about Leo."

For seven hours home, as we finally got through to the audiologist and made arrangements for her to look at Gommy's hearing aid, Leo crouched in his battered crate next to Joni in her pink one. He never made a sound. As soon as we got him to our house, he raced down the hall and hid under a bed.

I sent a photo of Leo to Vera, who shows it to Gommy whenever she asks about him. So far, she hasn't forgotten. Just the other night she badgered Vera into calling us, and demanded, "When am I getting my cat back?"

We didn't tell her that our daughter Caitlin had canvassed her friends and one of them had generously offered to take Leo. But when Leo's final bloodwork came in, it showed that in addition to the gum infection, he also has a major heart problem, hypertrophic cardiomyopathy, which Jeff suspected when he heard the heart murmur. He will need medication and careful care for the rest of his life. We couldn't in good conscience give such a sick cat to Caitlin's friend. Leo needs to live with a veterinarian. Leo needs to live with Jeff.

Gommy and Leo will miss each other deeply. It breaks my heart that they have to adapt to new homes without each other.

After a couple of weeks, Leo finally came out from under our bed and slept at the foot on Jeff's side. Lionman slept on my side, and Joni slept in between us.

Next month, we will help Gommy move to assisted living.

The Ruby Mirror

When our younger daughter Kelsey was a toddler, she thought the rearview mirror was called "the ruby mirror." She was quite disappointed to learn the prosaic and practical truth. It became a family tradition, when we piled in the car, to turn to each other and say, "Look in the ruby mirror!" We still invoke the ruby mirror sometimes now even though Kelsey is grown. It has become a metaphor for seeing the world in a more meaningful way.

I believe Kelsey as a toddler had this idea that when we referred to this mirror, we were talking about a special magical mirror made from rare jewels, like from a fairy tale, that might somehow show the truth. The ruby is my birthstone, so it has always had significance for me. I've read that rubies are relatively rare, that they can vary in color from a deep pink to the color of blood, and that rubies are believed to be the stone of passion, love, and a joy in life. They have been considered a symbol for powerful feelings.

Because of the word "ruby," Kelsey's phrase reminded me of the ruby slippers from *The Wonderful Wizard of Oz*. Of course, it also reminded me of the magic mirror in *Snow White*, when the evil queen asked, "Mirror, mirror, on the wall, who's the fairest of them all?" The term "ruby mirror" also reminds me of the expression to "look at the world through rose-colored glasses."

As I look back over our life so far in the ruby mirror, what do I see?

Before meeting each other, my husband and I both had fancy fairy-tale weddings to people we weren't prepared to live with. I had married a rebound guy, still nursing my breakup from my college boyfriend. My first marriage lasted about four years. Jeff had married a girl he knew was too wild and immature for him. His first marriage lasted only four months. Though we were lucky not to have children with our "starter marriages," the years following our divorces were so traumatic and lonely that when we found each other, and then when we had our children, we were over-the-moon ecstatic with our new little family. Looking through the ruby mirror, I see that if those starter marriages hadn't dissolved, we never would have met each other, and while we might have had other children, we would not have had Caitlin and Kelsey.

It wasn't that we didn't have fights. Once I smashed a dish on the floor. I can't even remember why I did it. During the early years of our marriage, we both had times where we took long, angry walks, didn't speak for hours, had fights about not going to bed angry. We had disagreements about the division of labor, as most couples do. We had arguments about religious training for our children, and about the existence of God and the afterlife. But both of us had been so scalded by our divorces that I believe there was an unspoken agreement that we would not go there again. We were in it for the long haul. I finally accepted that Jeff's job demanded so much of him that the lion's share of the parenting would be up to me.

The girls had a happy childhood, I think. When they were children we lived in a neighborhood with a sweet elementary school, right down the street from their father's veterinary clinic. Our daughters could visit nearly every day and pet dogs and cats of all colors and sizes. I was always coming up with art projects for them. In the basement at night, Jeff played guitar and the girls danced and played rock star with toy guitars of their own. They did soccer and basketball and gymnastics and the neighborhood pool was right around the corner. Caitlin loved our house in that neighborhood so much that she has kept track of every time it is bought and sold on Zillow. There were several years when she was making plans to move back there some day. They were able to see Jeff's parents and their cousins frequently, which made for many happy memories around Rosh Hashanah, Hanukkah, and Passover. And we visited my parents and brother and his family several times a year, never missing a Christmas.

I will admit that often my daughters and I, when they were little, spent Friday afternoons snuggling on the couch together watching *Swan Princess* or *Little Mermaid*. I myself loved getting swept away in those happily-ever-after movies, with both of the girls curled next to me, as I ran my fingers over their damp temples and through their silky curls.

I wonder, did I fill my daughters' heads with fairy-tale endings, not preparing them for the vicissitudes of life? Did they have a false fantastical, magical view of the world? They are both fun, generous, high-functioning and well-adjusted adults now, and I believe they would say the answer is no.

Seeing what's behind you—looking in the rearview mirror—can be an enlightening experience. Now, looking back and remembering our children's childhood is an unimaginably sweet experience for me. I actually surprised myself because I loved everything about being a mother and didn't expect to. I have always been a dreamy, absent-minded person who doesn't function well without sleep.

Not only did motherhood require practicality and alertness, and an almost constant ability to think on my feet, it also required me to function on only a few hours of sleep on a pretty consistent basis. It required the introverted non-cook me to interact constantly and to produce meals and snacks multiple times a day. To be decisive and authoritative. None of these were strengths of mine; nevertheless, in my rose-colored memory, I was blissfully happy during that time.

And so here we are, in our sixties. Jeff and I take long, companionable walks together now. We rarely raise our voices. We finish each other's sentences, and we have a comfortable routine. Jeff has retired, while I am still writing. We have close friends who mean a great deal to us. We stay active; we've traveled a little. We both try to nourish our creativity, Jeff by playing guitar and me by writing and learning new skills like painting. We try to do things for others. There is no one we'd rather be with than each other.

Both girls have satisfying careers, and they were both recently married in beautiful weddings to outstanding young men. We are so lucky to be able to see them frequently. The other night the girls and their husbands were here and we were standing around in the kitchen, finishing our wine after an early Thanksgiving dinner. Kelsey, our family playlist queen, put on "Uptown Funk" by Bruno Mars and suddenly we were all dancing. We danced and laughed and danced some more until we were just about ready to drop. I looked around at our family and thought, *I wish I could stop time right now and treasure this ecstatic moment.*

We've had some bad periods. We've experienced a miscarriage, cancer, mental health challenges, family feuds, career disappointments, and the losses of three of our parents. But the bad periods are hazy, and, over the arc of time, they have only served to sharpen the joy of the good. I will admit to deliberately viewing life through a positive lens. Looking in "the ruby mirror," I would say that we have had a precious life together indeed so far and feel so truly grateful.

The future? I watched my parents live devotedly, nearly attached at the hip, into their older years. In their mid-eighties their lives began to unravel. Both started to show signs of dementia. Mom had surgery for colon cancer. Dad had a tumor on his pancreas. After Dad passed away Mom was hopelessly lonely for him and really never recovered. For four years I cared for Mom, as she moved from independent living to assisted living to memory care in a blistering decline. She started out determined to make friends and ended up barely being able to make it to the bathroom.

As I cared for Mom, Jeff helped. He went with me to visit. He helped with her walker and wheelchair. He bought her candy and cut up her food for her. Toward the end he fed her like a child. Perhaps he, too, could see a future where we would need to do these things for each other. And now we are involved with the care of his mother, though his sister and her family are the primary caretakers.

We all need a ruby mirror. A way to count our blessings and to see the joy in life, to see our past experiences as the gems of our lives, and to embrace them all with passion, forgiveness, and gratitude.

Fixing Up Dr. Jeff

Dr. Jeff spent all his time helping sick animals. He mended their broken bones, gave them medicine, and watched over them in their hospital beds. Night after night his pets saw him eat a TV dinner and fall asleep reading a fat medical book.

"We need to fix him up," said Roosevelt one night. Roosevelt was a dog with three legs. Dr. Jeff had saved his life, and named him after Franklin D. Roosevelt, who didn't let his wheelchair stop him from being a great president.

"What's wrong with him?" asked Amelia, a canary with one wing. Dr. Jeff had saved her life, too, and named her after Amelia Earhart, a famous airplane pilot.

"I mean fix him up with someone to love," said Roosevelt.

Ludwig, Dr. Jeff's deaf white cat, didn't say anything. He was asleep on the piano. Dr. Jeff had named him after Ludwig Von Beethoven, a composer who didn't let deafness stop him from creating beautiful music. When he was awake, which wasn't very often, Ludwig ran up and down the piano keys, trying to watch the moon pass outside the window.

The next day, Roosevelt, Amelia, and Ludwig saw a TV program in which a charming lady showed people how to train dogs.

"We could fix Dr. Jeff up with her," said Roosevelt.

"Hmmm," said Amelia.

Ludwig didn't say anything. He was asleep on the piano.

That night, as always, Dr. Jeff ate his TV dinner and fell asleep on the couch with a medical book on his chest.

"We must take matters into our own paws," said Roosevelt.

"Wings," said Amelia.

"Whatever," said Roosevelt. "Tomorrow we'll go to the TV station and bring back the dog trainer lady."

"But we've never been outside without Dr. Jeff," said Amelia.

"The only thing we have to fear is fear itself," said Roosevelt.

The next day when Dr. Jeff went out for the newspaper, the three pets slipped out. They watched cars whiz by.

"I am a dog with three perfectly good legs," said Roosevelt bravely.

"Fears are paper tigers," said Amelia. Ludwig didn't say anything, but he watched Roosevelt and Amelia closely to make sure they didn't go anywhere without him.

And so they set off. Roosevelt was in the lead, with his uneven gait. Amelia followed, hop-flutter, hop-flutter, and Ludwig slunk behind.

On the way, a pigeon attacked Amelia, and Roosevelt had to bite off some of its tail feathers. Ludwig mistakenly walked into a revolving door and was pushed around three times before Roosevelt and Amelia could get him out.

When they finally arrived at the TV station, the dog trainer lady sat on a couch in the lobby crying into a lace handkerchief. One dog chewed her purse, and two more wrestled beside the elevator.

"I am not proud of any of you," said the dog trainer lady between hiccups. "If you weren't such bad dogs I would still have a TV show."

Roosevelt and Amelia felt sorry for her. Ludwig might have, too, but he was admiring his reflection in the glass door. When he practiced a graceful pounce, the dogs saw him. Amelia and Roosevelt heard loud barking as they tore across the lobby, trailing their leashes. They tried to warn Ludwig.

When Ludwig saw the dogs' reflections in the glass door, he puffed out every hair on his body and let out the loudest meow anyone had ever heard.

Every dog present gave its ears a good shake.

Then, to everyone's surprise, Ludwig swiped the biggest dog across the nose with one claw. Amelia pecked. Roosevelt snapped and dodged. Clumps of fur flew.

On her way to work, the afternoon talk-show host opened the door, and the bad dogs almost knocked her over running out. Then, a three-legged dog, a one-winged bird, and a cat ran the other direction. Three blocks later they ducked into an alley to rest.

"We need to fix Dr. Jeff up with someone *else*," said Roosevelt. His sides heaved and one paw was bleeding.

"I could not agree more," said Amelia. Her feathers were bedraggled.

Ludwig didn't say anything. He was taking a short nap.

That was when they saw a dirty kitten walking toward an open sidewalk grate.

"Watch out!" said Amelia.

The kitten stopped and listened. Then walked on. Roosevelt

raced to the grate's edge and nudged it away. Suddenly a slim freck-led hand scooped up the kitten.

"You poor little thing! I think you might be blind." The hand belonged to a small woman with a friendly face and fluffy blonde hair. "Does this kitten belong to you?" The woman patted Roosevelt on the head. He thumped his tail on the sidewalk. Ludwig rubbed against her leg and Amelia hopped onto her knee. "How nice to meet you all," she said.

And that was when Roosevelt, Amelia, and Ludwig led her hop-flutter, hop-flutter, all the way to Dr. Jeff's clinic.

"Where have you been?" Dr. Jeff said when they straggled into his waiting room. "I've been worried sick!"

"They saved this kitten's life," said the fluffy-haired woman.

"Hi." Dr. Jeff smiled.

"I think this kitten is blind," said the fluffy-haired woman.

Dr. Jeff kept smiling. "Blind animals do fine if you keep them inside and don't move your furniture."

"My landlady doesn't allow pets."

"Well . . . he can live here with us. Right, guys?" Dr. Jeff was talking to the animals but still smiling at the fluffy-haired woman.

"Wonderful!" she said.

"And you'll visit?"

And after that, Lisa (which was her name) came over for dinner nearly every night. Dr. Jeff stopped buying TV dinners. He got some good recipes from the dog trainer lady's new TV cooking show.

Lisa liked to paint, and often spread her paints and canvases on the table after dinner. One night, while Lisa painted, the kitten walked through her paints. She put paper down and let the kitten make paw print paintings. They named him Edgar, after Edgar Degas, an artist who kept painting after he lost his eyesight.

They made a cozy group in the evenings. Lisa and Edgar painted. Ludwig ran up and down the piano keys. Amelia sat on Dr. Jeff's shoulder, her spirits soaring, and Roosevelt stood guard.

In reading his medical books, Dr. Jeff fell only a little behind.

Acknowledgments

It has been a joy to put this collection together. My first idea was simply to collect the various essays that had been published over my life so that my children could access them easily in one place. Then, as I worked on the collection, I decided that I wanted to deepen and flesh out some of the themes that came up by adding more essays. About half of the essays have been published, while the rest are new. Those that have been previously published are listed inside the front cover, and I thank the publishers of those journals and magazines.

Jeff was my first reader, and he helped me with many of the memories. His delight in this voyage through the "ruby mirror" of our life together encouraged me to think this was a project worth pursuing. Caitlin and Kelsey's enthusiasm for the essays also encouraged me; I felt deeply rewarded by their interest, since this project is essentially for them.

Thank you to the dear and treasured members of my writers' groups—Liz Hatley, Michelle Moore, Emily Pearce, and Betsy Thorpe—whose thoughtful and insightful comments have helped me shape each essay and the overall collection. My long-time close friend, Ann Campanella, with her unerring poet's and editor's eye, gave me the gift of the three-part organizational scheme. Suzanne Leitner's thoughtful feedback helped me see where I needed to go deeper. Master memoirist Judy Goldman was so kind to read several of the essays, and to offer invaluable feedback on scene-setting, truth-telling, and reflection. My friend Mimi Krumholtz, an excellent reader, gave me encouragement, and my artist friend Catherine Mainous's enthusiastic support as well as artistic suggestions were greatly appreciated. Of course, huge thanks to Kelsey Kline Mard, my daughter, for her absolutely dreamy cover design.

Thank you to Diana Wade for her beautiful book design, and to Katherine Bartis for her sensitive copy-editing.

It has also meant the world to me to have dear author friends write blurbs for this collection—Ann Campanella, Rick Dresser, Judy Goldman, and Gilda Morina Syverson.

Finally, heartfelt thanks to all who take the time to read these glimpses into the "ruby mirror" of our life.

A medium which transports
story from inspiration to creation.
Our desire is that authors and readers
will be affirmed through
creativity and the written word.